Badass Mindfulness Cultivating Powerful Thinking and Manifesting Desires

Unleash Your Inner Wizard and Conquer
Your Thoughts With Style and Sass

PAULINE VINCENT

Table of Contents

Introduction

Has your mind ever felt like it won't stop racing or that it's stuck rehashing the past? Do worries about tomorrow hold you back today? You're definitely not alone there; so many people get tangled in thinking traps that prevent joy and achieving what they want. But it doesn't have to be this way forever. Your thoughts don't define you, and with some work, you can untangle your mind and rewrite your story. There are always ways to redirect where our brains wander, so we can start feeling free.

In these pages, I'll share simple tools to tame that chatty mind through mindfulness and positive manifestation. By the end, your view will change, and good things will grow. I'm Denise; I've always loved pushing myself through sports, like snowboarding in the terrain park. But I wanted to learn how I could improve myself and overcome that fear when riding in the park and doing tricks. Then I discovered freediving, which taught me the power of a calm mind. Learning breath control and presence underwater helped me apply those tools to snowboarding too. I learned how to focus and manifest a result. Sharing what I've learned with others in my freediving classes, I see how exploring your inner voice can transform stressful situations. Finding that deep sense of control comes from self-awareness and presence. Facing fears by positively channeling your thinking is so liberating. That's what drives me to keep learning and helping others do the same. Now I'm passing on those proven low-effort strategies so you can feel that wonderful self-control too!

Here are just a few of the benefits you can expect from reading this book:

- **Reduce stress and worry:** Say goodbye to hours spent anxiously overthinking the past or future. You'll learn simple rituals to shift your mindset to a more peaceful place.

- **Boost confidence and motivation:** Stop putting yourself down and start appreciating your talents. With the manifestation methods I share, you can achieve anything you set your mind to.

- **Improve relationships:** Clear your head of irrational jealousies, comparisons, or resentments. You'll deal with other people from a place of patience, understanding, and love.

- **Unlock creativity:** A cluttered mind can't think outside the box. But with mindfulness tools to find focus, you'll access a whole new level of original ideas.

- **Enhance performance:** My clients in high-pressure fields like sports use my strategies to stay centered under pressure. You'll thrive at work or school too with laser-like concentration.

- **Gain clarity:** No more confusion or second-guessing yourself. You'll see situations from a wise, balanced perspective, allowing you to make smart choices with ease.

- **Enjoy better health:** Studies show positive thinking supports well-being (Johns Hopkins Medicine, 2019). Reduce physical ailments by releasing mental and emotional tension at the root.

And that's just a teaser of what's possible. By the end of this book, you'll proudly own your thoughts and feel surefooted, navigating any challenge with composure. You'll float through each day confident, carefree, yet focused—basically, as the master of your own mindful magic!

Allow me to tell you a bit about myself and why I'm perfectly qualified to guide you on your mindfulness journey.

As someone who has studied both breathwork and neuroplasticity in-depth, I understand the science behind how our thoughts physically shape our brains and behaviors. Through years of personal experience transforming my own mindset, I've fine-tuned powerful yet simple techniques for cultivating a positive outlook.

My background didn't start in psychology, though. Early in my world travels, I discovered freediving, which opened my eyes to the profound connection between one's mental state and physical abilities. The more I learned, the more passionate I became about exploring this relationship further.

This led me to intensify my training in freediving, breathwork, and different meditative disciplines. I eventually became a respected instructor, sharing what I'd discovered with both recreational and competitive divers. Along the way, I also published my first book, "Relax for Waves," drawing on lessons from the sport.

But it was through working one-on-one with athletes and students and battling inner turmoil that I found my true calling. By helping them enhance focus, confidence, and coping skills, I saw firsthand how transformative developing "badass mindfulness" could be. This experience is what prompted me to write this current book.

Now, through my depth of knowledge combined with years of real-world application, I can fast-track you to mental mastery. You don't have to feel stressed or stuck any longer. I promise that if you commit to this book, you'll soon see yourself and your potential in an exciting new light.

No longer will you identify as a victim of circumstance. Instead, you'll proudly own your thoughts and walk tall, knowing that every day brings new opportunities when you approach life from a place of positivity and hope. Difficult times may still come, but they won't throw you off course when your default setting is optimistic, flexible thinking. You'll glide through obstacles with grace and ease.

So, if feeling more in control of your mind and happiness sounds appealing, this is the perfect book for you. Give it a try; it will be life-changing! Dive in and start your journey to becoming the master of mindfulness today. The future you have always wanted is closer than you think.

Chapter 1:

Setting the Stage

Jenny was stressed. As a working single mom, she felt like she was constantly struggling just to keep up. There never seemed to be enough hours in the day, and money was always tight. She dreamed of buying a house one day, but every time she tried to save up some cash, something would come along and wipe out her funds—a broken car, a sick kid, skyrocketing utility bills.

It was starting to feel hopeless. Jenny found herself lying awake almost every night, worrying about everything that could potentially go wrong. Her mind was constantly flooded with worst-case scenarios and doubts about whether things would ever get better. She just wanted some relief from the endless cycle of chaos and stress but didn't know where to even start trying to change her situation.

Sound familiar? Most people can relate to feeling overwhelmed like life is out of control. We get so caught up in all the problems and worries that we lose sight of happier times. It becomes way too easy to slip into patterns of negative thinking on autopilot. But here's the good news: you don't have to just accept feeling powerless and stuck. There are simple steps you can take to shift your mindset and start creating the life you want.

By learning to master our thoughts and feelings, we unlock the power to intentionally shape our reality. Does this idea of empowered manifestation seem too good to be true? I promise that, with the right understanding and practice, it works! Let me explain the core concepts.

First up, we need to establish a growth mindset. This means realizing that our habits and nature are not fixed; we have the power to intentionally change unwanted patterns through continuous effort. Our brains are naturally wired for survival-oriented negative thinking as a defense mechanism, but we can retrain ourselves to see opportunities instead of threats through consistent mindfulness work.

Now let's talk about manifestation itself. Simply put, it's the ability to deliberately impact external conditions by first changing our internal state. How we think and feel colors our entire experience of reality. When we assume the feeling of our wishes already being fulfilled, we energetically attract corresponding people and circumstances into alignment. It's not about empty positive confessions but a truly heartfelt shift from lack to abundance.

At the center of effective manifestation lies our intentions. We must have a laser focus on positive goals stated in the present tense as if they have already been achieved. Doubts and complaints will only undermine our efforts, so we need to monitor our thoughts for disempowering narratives and rewrite them in an aspiring tone. Affirmations can assist with this by priming our subconscious to expect good outcomes each day.

Thoughts lead to feelings, and feelings produce behaviors that shape our reality. So, the third key aspect of badass mindfulness is empowering emotions. We all naturally gravitate toward familiar emotions, whether constructive or not. But we can take charge and replace things like anxiety, anger, or sadness with uplifting alternatives through mindfulness tools. Simply focusing our attention on our breath improves our mood in minutes.

And finally, we unlock our innate inner wizard by trusting in our creative powers. Inside each of us lies a force of imagination and will that can actualize any vision when guided by positivity, persistence, and playfulness. This inner wisdom knows exactly what we need in each moment to keep optimizing our lives. By quieting doubts and focusing on potential, we give it room to work its magic on our behalf.

Mastering manifestation requires consciously replacing old thoughts with new aspirations stated confidently as present facts. We must proactively shift out of harmful feelings into elevated attitudes through mindfulness. And we unleash our innately magical ability to shape optimal outcomes by opening to life's flow with faith in favorable possibilities. With regular practice, this mindful magic creates amazing breakthroughs from even the smallest of daily efforts over time.

The Limitations of Conventional Positive Thinking

Positive thinking has undoubtedly become very popular in recent times. From motivational quotes shared daily on social media to the countless self-help books and seminars available, we're constantly encouraged to focus on the bright side and visualize our dreams coming true. And on the surface, there are good reasons for this approach's widespread adoption.

When we assume a sunny attitude, it intuitively feels like it would lead to better places emotionally and make life's struggles more bearable. Optimism also just sounds more pleasant than a constant complaint. Scientific research has linked positive thinking to health benefits like a lower risk of heart disease and a longer life (Tello, 2019). So, most people give positive affirmations and visualization techniques an enthusiastic try, hoping it will lighten their load and attract their goals.

And for many, conventional positive thinking methods do seem to help to some degree by lifting spirits in hard times. Regularly rehearsing uplifting self-talk trains our inner voice to lean more encouragingly over time. Just changing our internal channel from worries to aspirations provides temporary relief from negativity's grip. Visualizing accomplishments can spark imagination and fuel motivation to take action.

However, while conventional positive thinking clearly has certain benefits, it also contains some significant limitations if used as a one-stop solution. For starters, repetitively demanding happiness and success through affirmations alone may start to feel like fantasy rather than reality if tangible changes aren't followed. This can trigger deeper discouragement when the mental scripts fail to perfectly align with the facts on the ground.

Positive thinking also risks setting unrealistic expectations that are doomed to disappoint if not grounded in practical consideration of obstacles. We then harshly criticize ourselves for inevitable deviations toward more complex emotions like frustration. This type of perfectionism paralyzes momentum by breeding fear of imperfect action.

Moreover, affirming non-stop about victory may unintentionally promote an avoidance of challenges for fear of vulnerability. We bypass opportunities for growth by skirting discomfort and the effort that true progress demands. Half-hearted plans without full commitment rarely bear fruit when difficulties arise.

Most crucially, conventional positive thinking tends to concentrate only on thoughts without recognizing their equal role alongside feelings and physical activity. We rationalize repeated failure to actualize dreams as a personal flaw rather than a systemic issue, beating ourselves up further. But emotions and behaviors prove equally potent in either empowering our potential or sabotaging it.

These limitations show how positive self-talk in isolation may not sufficiently equip us to attain the desired change. Wishing into a void often resembles escapism more than true problem-solving and manifestation. Without accompanying emotional regulation strategies, we're left at the mercy of old thought patterns when stress hits.

Realistically, undesirable external factors like lack of financial means or toxic relationships thwart even the most determined optimist spinning in thought alone. Positive thinking risks seeming out of touch when not acknowledging structural barriers beyond individual control. This breeds simmering frustration that poisons the well over time.

At its worst, positive thinking transforms into empty positive confessions that fail to convince even ourselves, taking the place of authentic empowerment. A flimsy mask of joy leaves us vulnerable to falling back into self-blaming despair when life's messiness surfaces through rose-colored glasses. This mental treadmill repeats itself miserably.

So, while holding space for optimism serves us, positive thinking in isolation provides only a partial solution disconnected from context. If used this way, it may even backfire and worsen problems through setting unrealistic expectations, avoiding challenges, or ignoring wider limitations. For growth to take root, we need integrative strategies incorporating thoughts, feelings, and actions in harmony.

Rather than empty affirmations, we require mindfulness practices to fortify presence, resilience, and agency. Emotions like anxiety or anger held for long reveal insights into underlying beliefs restricting our potential. Only by addressing the root causes of suffering through patient self-reflection can we find true inner freedom and empowerment. This compassionate inner work cultivates an empowered optimism grounded in reality.

With an understanding of positive thinking's limitations and by broadening our toolbox, we gain true mastery over how experiences shape our mindsets and destinies. Thoughts, feelings, and deeds all deserve conscious guidance. In this well-rounded system, we unlock unlimited possibilities while still treasuring life's rich complexities. Isn't that vision worth continuing our exploration?

The Power of Badass Mindfulness

We've seen some of the limitations of conventional positive thinking when used in isolation. While optimism remains crucial, we need a more holistic system that leverages our full potential as mind-body-spirit beings. This is where badass mindfulness truly shines as an evolutionary practice.

Badass mindfulness and manifestation recognizes the profound connection between our inner mental and emotional states and subsequent outer experiences. It's based on the understanding that our dominant thoughts and feelings literally shape our realities through subtle energetic influences. By consciously regulating and upgrading our internal channels, we take back the reins of creation from autopilot negative patterns.

This approach relies less on pep talks alone and more on tapping deep presence, clarity, and composure through tools like meditation. With calm focus, we gain insight into the conditioning limiting us unconsciously. As beliefs, attitudes, and emotional patterns reveal themselves, we gain room for empowered choice over what to accept and what needs replacing.

This inner work cultivates a vibrant flow state where inspiration, intuition, and imagination flourish. From that space of connection, our intentions gain the potency to manifest outward change through a mysterious blend of skill, serendipity, and synchronicity. Rather than superficially hoping, we patiently align with life's natural currents toward blossoming potential.

Numerous scientific studies now prove just how intimately our mental processes affect physical reality (Collins, 2018; Sanfey, 2023). Thoughts trigger biochemical reactions influencing health, gene expression, and even aging. Placebo pills can sometimes cure an illness purely because the patient expects healing (Kihlstrom, 2008). Conversely, stress hormones released in distressing conditions like trauma disrupt immune function.

On a subtle level, persistent feelings literally shape the energetic structures of our lives. When we hold beliefs about scarcity for a long time, more supporting events seem to materialize, confirming those fears through filters of perception. But by shifting the lens to faith in abundance and growth, corresponding opportunities magnetically shift into focus. It's a real "thoughts become things" phenomenon.

There are endless examples where badass mindfulness has unveiled hidden talents, healed damaged relationships, or manifested dream jobs seemingly out of the blue. Often, these breakthroughs arrive just when faith in possibilities somehow outgrows doubt's weakening grip through presence practice. From Olympic gold medals to publishing success stories, mindset transformation precedes external shifts.

Mary, a professional, experienced badass mindfulness's power personally after years of feeling stuck in a dreary career. Meditation gradually softened her rigid beliefs, like, "It's too late to change paths now." As limiting views dissolved, inspiration unfolded, bringing to light the idea that she had a talent for ocean conservation. Confidently visualizing impact awakened unexpected mentors who sponsored her freedom to train as an activist full-time through their groups.

Manifestation also healed a strained family bond for Mary. Recognizing that resentments only harmed her, she quietly shifted to unconditional care through each mindfulness session. Gradually, communication thawed and understanding blossomed where there was once confusion. A heartfelt talk bridged divisions, and today her relationship is stronger than ever before.

Stories like these show how consciousness shapes matter when guided by calm focus, resilience, and creative visioning anchored in self-knowledge. Manifestation empowers taking the wheel of destiny rather than feeling tossed helplessly by waves of chance. It gives us agency to consciously determine our stories' unfolding from moment to moment.

This doesn't mean positive confessions alone transform external conditions magically overnight. However, dedicated inner work cultivates frequencies, attracting supportive events that align with our upgraded essence and priorities over time. Manifestation blossoms naturally from seeds of empowered choice planted through such mindful magic's gentle cultivation. Its potential seems limitless when integrated with patience and faith in life's rhythms.

Setting Intentions with Purpose

We've seen how badass mindfulness relies on aligning our inner states with positive outcomes. A key part of this process involves deliberately selecting energized intentions rooted deeply in what we truly want and value. Rather than vague wishes, clear intentions act as guideposts, empowering conscious strides toward fulfillment.

But crafting effective intentions requires finesse. Just declaring desires halfheartedly with fingers crossed rarely sparks tangible change on its own. So, let's explore intention setting's nuances to take full advantage of its transformative powers.

First, we must clarify the root drivers behind our wants through self-inquiry. Do ambitions stem from authentic passions or feelings of lack? Intentions borrowing from others' standards rarely energize as powerfully. Taking time alone to reflect reveals the heart's true priorities beyond surface reasons or conditioned goals.

Next, transform general aspirations into specific, measurable intentions stated as present-tense achievements. Vaguely hoping for "more money someday" holds little directive force. But determining to earn $5,000 within six months through a side business sparks detailed plans and persistence. Be as precise as circumstances allow to charge intentions with tangible energy.

Also, ensure your intentions align with your highest good and won't harm others. Well-meaning but misguided desires sometimes miss life's lessons or bigger pictures. Intentions rooted in service, contribution, and personal growth tend to flow most effortlessly with life's currents over selfish gains alone. Aligning with higher purposes multiplies manifestation potency.

It further helps to set a timeframe with target dates before which you'll actualize your intentions. Whether you intend to learn guitar within a year or quit smoking by next spring, deadlines fuel passion and focus to overcome obstacles standing in the way. Time targets help anchor ephemeral hopes as real, achievable milestones.

Additionally, remain flexible and willing to alter intentions when the need arises. Rigidly clinging to plans out of ego even as signs point elsewhere cripples manifestation. Embrace fluidity by fine-tuning intentions in response to guidance from life experiences. Stay anchored to core values but adaptable to changing tides.

Tie intentions to corresponding actions and self-care routines. Dreaming alone affects little if not paired with daily work, which puts wheels in motion. Discipline in areas like education, finances, relationships, or exercise harmonizes intentions' frequency for outer achievement to smoothly follow. Make lifestyle-back intentions to amplify outcomes.

With some examples, let's synthesize these guidelines into sample intentions: "By February, I will publish my short story collection and earn $2,000 in royalties through marketing by hiring a freelance marketer. To actualize this, I will write 1,000 words daily and create social media promotions weekly while nourishing creativity through yoga."

Setting intentions and making a plan—when to do what—this way—with purpose, specificity, alignment, timeframes, and accompanying actions—supercharges our manifestation potential. It distinguishes nebulous hopes from potent guiding forces steering each moment toward fulfillment. Now it's your turn to craft some meaningful intentions by applying these best practices for transformative results!

Chapter 2:

The Psychology Behind

Manifestation

To truly maximize manifestation's potential, we must appreciate its psychological underpinnings. After all, having dreams often achieves little without fathoming the subtle mechanisms behind achieving goals in reality.

Understanding the psychology guiding our thoughts, feelings, and behaviors empowers us to take active control. It provides a map of how inner workings motivate external actions and events through invisible energetic ties. Recognizing these linkages lets us optimize behaviors supporting manifestation while minimizing those sabotaging it. Knowledge transforms us from passive wishers to architects shaping our realities.

So, let's delve into some key psychological drivers powering manifestation from behind the scenes. Exploring mind-body mechanisms illuminates previously hidden leverage points for positive change. It sheds light on why certain attitudes seem to attract abundance while others spell scarcity despite identical circumstances on paper. With this awareness, our intentions gain microscopic precision, guiding circumstances.

First up, how we view others affects our realities through projection biases. People tend to subconsciously spot the same traits in others they secretly judge in themselves, whether positive or negative. If we harbor inner resentment, such criticism colors perceptions, fueling self-fulfilling conflict.

By releasing judgment and assuming the best in people through compassion, we flip this tendency, which operates unconsciously from day to day. Affirming others' inherent goodness uplifts all relationships while generating cooperation instead of conflict. This positive projection empowers cooperative manifestation through aligned interactions.

Our self-image holds equal potency in destiny's unfolding. Think of iconic figures attaining seemingly impossible goals against all odds solely due to an undying belief in their inherent talents. Their unshakeable self-worth fueled perseverance through temporary defeats when others surrendered. Intuition, creativity, and opportunity stemmed from this rock-solid foundation.

Comparatively, harboring limiting views like "I'm no good at math" or "My family isn't successful" subtly shapes interests, effort levels, and outlook, attracting events confirming such fears. But infusing ourselves with unconditional self-love, respect, and possibility-seeking transforms this inner blueprint with ripple effects. As Einstein said, imagination shapes reality more than knowledge alone ever can.

Another driver lies in how we interpret challenges, from traffic jams to health setbacks. Seeing obstacles as personal failings and signs of lack or doom commonly breeds fear, tension, and giving up. But reframing difficulties as inevitable parts of growth and preparing us for greater paths ahead shifts reaction into opportunity-finding determination. Any stumble feels less discouraging, knowing it builds character rather than defines worth.

Our beliefs around scarcity and abundance exert powerful control through perceptual filters too. If shortage feels normal despite apparent excess all around, experiences validate this mindset unconsciously. Resources seem insufficient, no matter the actual amounts, due to fear-colored glasses. However, shifting the lens to a natural abundance mindset magnetizes corresponding nurturing events while easing the need to clutch or compete unhealthily for scraps.

Even deep-rooted social conditioning like gender stereotypes limits potential and shapes our manifestation destiny through self-fulfilling demotivation. Any preconceived notion of limitations subtly constricts choices and drives outcomes toward conforming truths as a form of self-defense against threats to the ego. However, recognizing and discarding inherited biases creates permission to color outside prescribed lines with boundless creativity.

On the granular level, our moment-to-moment thoughts form essential mental soil, either stunting manifestation or blossoming it. Positive thinking literally primes brain circuitry for happier outlooks through neuroplasticity over time. But negative ruminations conversely cement distressing perspectives through the repetitive firing of certain neural pathways.

With these insights, we can now appreciatively guide our inner GPS toward beneficial mindsets that support joy and abundance. Negative thought-catching consciously flips scripts toward potential-focused visions with patience. Soon, external realities will mirror the optimized patterns running our new internal software through feedback loops between consciousness and physics.

So, while manifestation arises from unified intentions, psychology, emotion, and actions over longer arcs, its unseen mind mechanisms ultimately determine upward or limited trajectories. Understanding excavates buried treasures of insight and choice, transforming lives. What other hidden levers for positive change have you spotted that intrigue exploring deeper to optimize your manifestation potential? Stay tuned as we unpack further keys to mastering mind-body synergy for intended growth!

The Subconscious Mind: The Gatekeeper of Manifestation

We've explored the conscious choices and mindsets directing manifestation through intention and psychology. But a deeper force orchestrates much of what we experience on autopilot below awareness—our subconscious. So, understanding its inner workings is key to optimizing manifestation practically without effort.

Simply put, the subconscious is the non-thinking aspect of the mind, storing all memories, behaviors, and attitudes formed since birth through its processing hub, the amygdala. From unconscious biases to relationship patterns, this databank shapes our filters and automatic reactions outside of awareness. Its sheer processing speed far outpaces conscious reasoning, determining how we navigate each moment before we even know it.

Given its primal importance in governing survival instincts, the subconscious evolved not to question preprogrammed responses but to obey them diligently for protection. However, this also means taking its directions as absolute truths without considering alternative viewpoints that could serve us better. Its sole role involves efficiently reacting rather than higher-order creative decision-making.

Unfortunately, many subconscious beliefs fueling behaviors stem from childhood experiences before developing rational faculties. Whether loving or traumatic, early imprinting leaves deep foundations for how we view the world, which the subconscious fiercely defends as reality, even if it is maladaptive now. So, without consciously reexamining its directives, old programming directs our ship long after helming abilities have matured.

This prebuilt software defines what feels possible versus impossible according to its databank alone, making the subconscious the ultimate barrier or boost for manifestation. If we hold negative self-schemas like "I'm unlucky" or "relationships always fail me," it ensures attracting valid evidence for protection no matter our intentions. Its commands override conscious optimism through emotional and perceptual filters.

Similarly, distressing past relationships or events etch subconscious fears into behaviors through memories, which, if unaddressed, guarantee sabotaging current progress to avoid perceived threats. No positive affirmation can shift outcomes unless paired with rewriting its core rulebook, as conscious will hold little authority compared to its directives executed each instant automatically.

We can access the subconscious to optimize programming through mindfulness, meditation, hypnotherapy, and similar reimprinting tools. By bypassing analytical reasoning and speaking directly to its language of images, feelings, and stories, we gently update outdated schemas and replace anxious patterns with empowering choices liberated from past constraints.

With patience and compassion, exploring the root causes of ingrained schemas and replacing limiting views with beneficial alternatives updates the subconscious GPS. Old restrictive beliefs dissolve without threats to the fragile ego, freeing remarkable untapped potential and resculpting reality according to an upgraded essence. Now the subconscious aids manifestation rather than obstructing through outdated firewalls rooted in the past rather than presence.

So, subconscious directives govern our autopilot beyond reasoning, determining what feels within reach. Its rules originate from childhood and traumatic experiences. By reexamining maladaptive programming compassionately, we regain authority, guiding its immense powers to serve the highest good versus past fears. With this insight, limitless vistas are truly open to consciously designing the reality field.

Breaking Free From Limiting Beliefs and Blocks

We've seen how deeply ingrained beliefs directed by our subconscious shape manifestation potential through perceptual filters and self-fulfilling assumptions. However, some of this programming no longer empowers us as adults due to outdated circumstances or misguided conditioning from unreliable sources. Recognizing when beliefs limit rather than liberate our potential represents the first step in dissolving constraints.

Limiting beliefs essentially reflect opinions we accept as unquestionable truths about ourselves or life that sabotage goals through self-doubt, fear, or hesitation to act. Common examples involve thinking "I'm not good enough," believing "success requires sacrificing happiness," or harboring notions that certain paths simply "aren't for people like me."

But where do these restricting beliefs originate? Often, early experiences instill distorted schemas beyond reason, like "if I achieve,

I'll lose love," due to conditional parenting. Societal stereotypes reinforced by insensitive role models can also leave toxic imprints that define worth through external markers alone. And traumatic past failures condition fears of vulnerability that must be avoided at all costs.

Some more common sources from which limiting beliefs arise are:

- Critical parents or caregivers who constantly put us down or say we won't be able to do things.

- Experiences of failure or rejection in the past make us believe we are not good enough.

- Comparing ourselves to others and feeling inferior.

- Strict rules we had to follow as kids that now restrict our choices.

- Overly traumatic events from the past that we keep remembering.

Our tendency to seek flaws while overlooking talents due to bias also fuels diminished self-views. Plus, peer pressure, comparison, and "the grass is greener" mindsets breed dissatisfaction by demanding unrealistic standards of perfection. The bottom line is that our programming comes from many unreliable sources, whereas trust in our divine spark transcends all judgment alone.

So, how can we update restricting filters into enlivening compasses? Journaling brings clarity by reflecting on the origins and impact of limiting narratives. Visualization mentally reframes obstacles as solvable rather than roadblock-defining stories. Daily cognitive exercises intentionally catch and flip negative tape loops. And reframing reconditions judgments as opportunities rather than personal failures.

Surrounding ourselves with inspirational mentors uplifts our views, whereas a toxic company drags down potential by confirming doubts as okay. Mindfulness removes us from reactive thoughts' thrall into presence's expansive vision. Setting micro-accomplishments builds momentum, proving self-deceptions as just that rather than facts.

Additionally, cognitive behavioral therapy provides tools to question automatically accepted beliefs while affirming inherent worth beyond the opinions of others. Recognizing that we simply mislabeled preferences or priorities as limitations also expands identities' flexibility. Gratitude softens scarcity filters by appreciating the abundance already surrounding us.

No matter our roots, we all deserve to support our divine rights, manifesting freely without outdated restraints from past shadows dimming present potentials. With patience and compassion, limiting beliefs dissolve and are replaced with empowering assumptions stated as facts. We become shapers of identity and capable sculptors, carving each moment according to upgraded essences no longer chained by fear or self-doubt masquerading as truth.

Exercises to Reprogram the Subconscious for Success

Our conscious mind is like the tip of an iceberg; it only sees a small part of what's really going on below the surface in our subconscious mind. That's why we often have the desire to change but find ourselves stuck in the same patterns. Or we try something new with motivation, but our old doubts creep back in. This is because the subconscious is very influential yet works outside our awareness.

The key is to consistently feed the subconscious with new, empowering information so it starts to replace old, unhelpful programs over time. The following are some powerful daily exercises anyone can do to reprogram their subconscious mind for success:

Morning Affirmations

Say positive statements about yourself out loud when you wake up and before bed. Phrase them in the present tense, like "I am confident" or "I effortlessly attract opportunity." This implants empowering beliefs into your subconscious while you're most receptive. Start with five minutes and work up to 15–20 minutes daily.

Creative Visualization

Take 10 minutes upon waking to visualize your ideal day unfolding with colorful, emotive details. See yourself handling situations with poise, radiating confidence, and achieving your goals. Imagine conversations, interactions, and feelings of accomplishment. This imprints the neural pathways for success.

Gratitude Journaling

Spend 15 minutes journaling things you're grateful for—people, opportunities, health, talents, nature, and so forth. Appreciate simple pleasures as well as big blessings. Gratitude shifts focus from lack to abundance, opening you up to more good things. Keep notes to refer to when doubts surface.

Nighttime Reviews

As you drift off, mentally replay your day's events, reframing any challenges in a positive, learning-focused way. For example, "I struggled with task X, but now that I see area Y, I can improve." This turns setbacks into springboards, both consciously and subconsciously.

Empowering Playlists

Curate an uplifting music playlist and listen for at least 30 minutes daily while doing other activities. Positive music lifts your mood naturally through the subconscious. Include songs with inspiring lyrics that match your goals.

Daily Affirmation Cards

Write your most meaningful affirmations on notecards to carry with you everywhere as reminders. Refer to a card when negativity creeps in to counteract those thoughts and shift your vibration upwards immediately. Place them in high-traffic areas at home as well.

Writing Exercises

Take 10 minutes during breaks to write about how you want to feel and what you want to achieve without conscious thought or censorship. This allows your subconscious wisdom to surface for exploration. Common themes offer insight and direction for consciously manifesting your potential.

Creative Problem-Solving

Schedule short creative periods like sketching, crafting, playing music, or other artistic hobbies that let your unconscious mind work beneath the surface. Novel ideas, inventions, and solutions often appear in this relaxed yet engaged state. Have notebooks handy to capture them for use in achieving life goals.

Gratitude Expressions

Send handwritten thank-you notes to people, past mentors, or even your future self, affirming your qualities, potential, and faith in your path. The very act of writing strengthens those neural connections. Keep notes you receive for tough times as subconscious reassurance.

Positive Self-Talk

Train yourself to automatically meet doubts or negatives with a confident positive contradiction stated in the present tense. For example, "I'm overwhelmed and lost" becomes "I calmly assess options and opportunities and gain clarity each day." Do this out loud until it becomes natural, so it reframes challenges consciously and subconsciously.

The Daily Review

Set aside 10–15 minutes at the end of each day to mentally review your day's experiences while relaxing. Reframe setbacks positively and see growth opportunities. Notice the small wins and times when your higher self-guided you well. File away lessons to strengthen what worked and release doubts into positive intentions for tomorrow.

Making these exercises part of your daily routine is key to sustainably reprogramming old, limiting beliefs and patterns over time. While consistency takes practice, you'll start attracting new opportunities and achieving goals more effortlessly as your dominant vibration rises. Celebrate each small shift; remember, change happens gradually below the surface before manifesting in your world. Commit to your success and keep feeding your subconscious mind, empowering new codes to live by.

The Neuroscience of Positive Thinking and Manifestation

Our brains are amazing organs that have the ability to change and adapt, even as adults. This trait is called neuroplasticity; it refers to how our experiences, thoughts, and behaviors can actually rearrange the physical connections between neurons in the brain. Neuroplasticity gives us the power to reshape our mindset and reprogram negative thinking patterns over time. Understanding its role is key to mastering manifestation through positive thinking techniques like visualization and affirmations.

Inside our brains are nerve cells called neurons that communicate with each other through connections called synapses. Our genes determine the basic framework, but the number and strength of these neural connections depend greatly on our experiences from birth onward. The more a connection is activated, the thicker and more myelinated it becomes for quicker future firing. The ones used less can even fade away, leaving traces of our unique thoughts and behaviors physically imprinted on our very brain structure.

This is why our environment and upbringing have such an influence on our beliefs and temperament. It's also why habits and addictions form—repeating the same thought patterns literally carves those grooves deeper. But the encouraging part is, we can form new grooves just as easily. Any time we learn a new skill or adapt to change, new synaptic connections are made and reinforced through practice until they become automatic. This ongoing neural remodeling is neuroplasticity in action.

Visualization takes advantage of neuroplasticity by vividly imagining our goals as if they have already been achieved. When we visualize success, promotions, relationships, or any positive scenario in vibrant sensory detail, the same neurons fire as if we're truly experiencing it. This repetitive activation strengthens those synaptic connections to physically shape the brain's wiring. Our subconscious doesn't distinguish between imagination and reality, so envisioning heights conditions us to self-fulfill the prophecy through confident action and drawing opportunities to us.

Similarly, affirmations recalibrate our thinking by repeating empowering, present-tense statements about ourselves and our abilities. Each time we say or think things like "I am talented and deserving," we stimulate the neurons tied to that concept to form denser networks, reinforcing our self-worth. Over time, it replaces the limiting tapes that once kept us stuck. Affirmations even activate the reticular activating system linked to motivation and perseverance, keeping us on track through challenges or setbacks.

Studies show that visualizing a physical task activates the same motor cortex areas as actual performance (Gabriele et al., 1989; Jeannerod, 1995). Learning while awake also strengthens the same neural pathways used during sleep for consolidation, so daytime practice pays off with increased ability and confidence upon waking. Simply pondering our goals stimulates the memory and reward regions, enticing us to take steps and bring them closer with each passing day.

The most compelling evidence is how affirmations impact the amygdala, a key structure regulating emotions and stress responses (Koosis, 2023). Repeated positive self-talk can actually rewire the brain's processing of threats over months and help manage fear. This shows how we truly shape our brain responses through mindful speech and reshaping limiting belief patterns; understanding neuroplasticity gives that power context.

Manifesting requires a growth mindset focused on potentials rather than impossibilities. Visualization and affirmations harness neuroplasticity to remold neural networks, representing ourselves as whole, capable beings who create opportunities. With consistency, their reinforcement leaves a permanent rearrangement underlying enduringly raised self-worth, motivation, and the ability to actualize all life has to offer. So, keep practicing positivity; you're nourishing your very brain each step of the way.

Neuroplasticity explains our innate ability to change through focused effort. By understanding its role, we gain conscious control over rewiring thought patterns that obstruct fulfillment. Visualization and affirmations directly leverage this process to strengthen qualities and impulses aligned with our highest good. In this scientific context, commitment to self-development feels even more empowering.

The Mind-Body Connection

Have you ever noticed that how you feel mentally affects your physical well-being and vice versa? Our minds and bodies are deeply intertwined in fascinating ways that impact our ability to achieve goals and feel our best. This relationship between the invisible processes of our mind and the visible workings of the body is known as "the mind-body connection." Understanding this profound interconnection is key to optimizing health, resilience, and the manifestation process.

The interface of mind and body holds immense power because what goes on internally gets externalized as experiences, relationships, and outer conditions. Stress, loneliness, or confidence aren't just felt; they produce physiological ripple effects influencing our energy levels, immunity, and general functioning without us always realizing it. Meanwhile, bodily discomforts like lingering illness can drain mental sharpness or buoyancy too if left unaddressed. It's a two-way exchange where each is dependent on the other for balance.

Modern science reveals anatomic links between the brain's limbic system, which controls our emotions, and the body's endocrine system, which releases hormones like cortisol that modulate stress responses (Kong et al., 2021). Long-term stress takes a physical toll by disrupting metabolism, aggravating illnesses, and inflaming tissues. Happier emotions, conversely, support cortisol regulation for health protection. Brain chemistry and neuronal activity can even shape gene expression via epigenetic imprinting over time. This cascading influence illustrates how strongly mindset permeates our cells.

Another key connection is via the autonomic nervous system split between the fight-or-flight stimulated sympathetic branch and the restorative parasympathetic half. Negative thinking keeps the former active, tensing muscles and raising blood pressure—we literally stress ourselves out! Whereas positive routines like exercise, creative hobbies, and deep breathing help shift into the soothing parasympathetic mode to let go of tension for rejuvenation. This leads to a calmer baseline that safeguards organs and speeds healing from within.

The spiritual dimension further amplifies the union between the psyche and physicality. An inner sense of purpose with meaning gives life coherence that strengthens the presence of mind and cellular resilience against chronic low-level stress from overwhelm or lack of fulfillment. Meditation cultivates focused stillness too, enhancing immunity, memory, and mind-body coordination through gamma brainwaves synchronizing both hemispheres.

Such psychological and biological interlacing means manifestation depends as much on internal attitudes and energetic states of being as outward action. Resisting thoughts of lack via gratitude and visualizing ideal outcomes reconditions the brain and cellular environment for abundance to materialize. Daily mindfulness, balanced routines, stress relievers, and social interaction prevent the stuck vibration that strains health and blocks new opportunities. Treating the mind and body as cooperative teammates optimizes vital force for manifestation.

From a holistic perspective, each individual is a co-creative spirit inhabiting a vessel of intelligence, emotions, physicality, and intuition, all mixed together in delicate homeostasis. Our well-being depends on nurturing each facet for synergy toward fulfillment. This explains why changing scenery, dumping negative relationships, or pursuing hobbies that provide flow states effectively recalibrate mood, energy levels, and consequently every part of our reality.

The mind-body principle reveals life as an artistic co-creation, not a series of events happening to us. How we perceive circumstances forms biological realities within, which shape further happenings through the invisible cues we project. Small adjustments in self-care, outlook, and daily focus yield exponential ripples of wellness that pave the way for dreams to materialize on their own accord. Remember, as within, so without. Your health awakens higher potential with each loving thought.

Our bodies are living temples for carrying minds on a lifelong, unfolding journey. Cultivating mindfulness of their profound unity empowers wise stewardship and co-creation from a place of wholeness. This nourishment liberates more spiritual qualities and abilities to gracefully weather the changes that come with each season of life.

Connection to the infinite through gratitude in each moment keeps the mind-body channel clear for life's bounty to continually flow your way.

The Power of Intention and Alignment

Have you ever noticed that some days just seem to flow more productively while others feel like an uphill battle? Much of this comes down to how focused and aligned our intentions are with the way we think, feel, and behave from moment to moment. Intention is the invisible energy guiding our manifestation power, so it's important to understand its role and cultivate congruence across all levels of our being.

In simple terms, intention refers to our conscious purpose, goals, or the driving force behind our choices in any given situation. It stems from a combination of desire, imagination, and free will working together. Our intentions direct our vital life force toward what truly matters: Shaping the future as we'd like it to unfold. This makes clarifying intention the vital first step for bringing dreams into form through dedicated action.

While desires remain hopes, intentions provide momentum by coupling dreams with a commitment to see them actualized. Pure intention doesn't waver or make exceptions for doubts; it holds the unwavering vision that pulls potential into present reality through our natural creative abilities. Like a focused lens concentrating sunlight to start a fire, intention gathers our energy into a laser-sharp channel for manifestation.

The mind-body principle reveals that our emotional states and habitual outlook also influence the wiring and biochemistry that govern energy levels, resilience, decision-making, and consequently, the outcomes we attract day by day. When mindset contradicts intention, it dilutes the power behind aspirations by creating inner conflict. However, alignment amplifies intention by maximizing every aspect of our being for success.

One key to mastering intention is congruence—making sure thoughts, feelings, and actions uniformly support chosen goals rather than working against each other. This means consciously catching negative thought patterns and reframing them with empowering perspectives. It's expressing gratitude daily instead of entitlement. Prioritizing relaxation to harness willpower instead of floundering in stress or distraction. Loving self-care nurtures a resilient, passionate vessel for high intentions to flow through as natural results.

Taking time each morning to visualize and feel the fulfillment of intentions sets the right emotional tone as well. Strong positive emotions broaden mindsets, strengthen relationships, and boost health in tangible ways correlated with success and satisfaction in life. Daily intention-setting establishes meaning, direction, and an upbeat internal climate conducive to achievement. These aligned energies then attract complementary events and new growth each following day.

The law of attraction also suggests we naturally guide situations toward harmonic alignment with our inward state on unconscious levels. This means high-level thinking with congruent intention helps resolve problems creatively as they surface in daily life, allowing higher outcomes to organically fall into place with less effort when the timing's right. By radiating confidence, we influence others to see opportunities where they previously saw limitations.

Overall, intention is like the magnetic North guiding life's navigational tools. When spirit, mind, and body stay congruently pointed to our highest vision despite obstacles, we maximize magnetism, drawing circumstances toward fruition at their perfect moment. This harmonic intention keeps us centered, resolute, and optimistic during uncertainty, so fulfillment remains inevitable. Alignment is the power multiplying intention's potential manifestation many times over!

Intention backed by congruence across all aspects of being best utilizes our inherent creative powers. It provides invisible direction and momentum, propelling us toward increasing well-being, abundance, and contributions aligned with our soul's purpose. Maintaining aligned intention through daily mindfulness keeps us grounded yet open to life's rich possibilities. With practice, it becomes second nature, so each day naturally falls into a grand master plan of personal and planetary evolution. Our highest dreams await such focus!

Chapter 3:

Thoughts vs. Thinking—

Understanding the Difference

Have you ever stopped to wonder—what exactly is the difference between random thoughts that pop into our heads all day compared to our actual thinking processes? There is an important distinction between the two that can greatly impact our ability to manifest.

We've all experienced the constant stream of thoughts that seem to flow endlessly in our minds. Thoughts just appear spontaneously without us even realizing it at first. Things like worries about the future, reminiscing about the past, and mental criticism of ourselves or others—these are examples of random thoughts. Studies show that, on average, we can have anywhere from 12,000 to 60,000 thoughts per day (Antanaityte, n.d.)! Most of the time, we are not even aware of what we are thinking because it happens automatically in the background of our minds.

These unfocused thoughts do not require much mental energy or intention. They simply arise on their own, without any real control or direction from our conscious minds. Because of this, many of the thoughts we have day-to-day do not necessarily reflect our true interests, values, or goals. They can sometimes contradict what we consciously wish to manifest. So, if manifestation stems from focused intention and direction of thoughts, these random, unfocused thoughts do not necessarily help the process.

Thinking, on the other hand, involves more conscious mental effort and awareness. When we choose to actively think about something, it requires engaging different parts of the brain related to memory, problem-solving, rationality, and language processing. Thinking allows us to purposefully direct our focus toward a specific outcome we want, rather than letting thoughts stray aimlessly. It gives us power over our mental processes, versus being at the mercy of random mind chatter all the time.

One key difference between thoughts and thinking is intent. Random thoughts lack a sense of purpose or goal behind them. But when we actively think about something, there is a conscious intent to explore, analyze, or manifest a certain outcome. Our thoughts may be about past regrets or worries, but thinking can steer the mind toward envisioning future solutions and success instead. Another major contrast is attention: thoughts scatter our focus, while focused thinking keeps the mind narrowly focused on one topic at a time.

Understanding this distinction is so important for manifestation because it shows how to direct mental energy purposefully where it will yield results rather than letting it run wild. When we catch our mind generating unhelpful thoughts, we can consciously choose to override it with productive thinking patterns aligned with our goals instead. Thinking helps us avoid getting drawn into the drama of random thoughts and break limiting patterns holding us back.

By practicing catching those unfiltered mental commentaries before they grasp you and substituting goal-focused thinking instead, your manifestation results can obtain a new level of precision and frequency.

Defining Thoughts and Thinking Processes

To understand the difference between thoughts and thinking processes, we must first define what thoughts are exactly. In simple terms, thoughts can be described as ideas, images, memories, or mental conversations that arise continuously in our consciousness. They are the basic contents of our stream of awareness that we have little direct control over. Thoughts arise automatically and spontaneously in response to both external stimuli as well as our internal experiences, feelings, and memories.

While thoughts often relate to emotions we're experiencing in the present moment, they are differentiated from emotions themselves. Emotions involve physiological reactions in the body along with feelings, whereas thoughts are primarily mental contents that can trigger emotions but are not the same thing. Similarly, thoughts differ from actual sensations or perceptions through the five senses occurring in the physical realm. Our thoughts may reference or comment on sensations, but they exist on an abstract, conceptual level within the mind itself.

Some key aspects that further characterize the nature of thoughts include:

- Thoughts tend to be reactive and conditioned by past experiences, rather than original or creative.

- They often arise involuntarily, without conscious effort or intention guiding them.

- The contents of thoughts are broad-ranging, transient images and verbalizations that flow continuously in response to both external and internal factors.

- We typically have little awareness or control over the specific thoughts arising in each moment, as opposed to the thinking processes, we consciously engage in.

Now let's look at thinking processes in contrast. Thinking involves conscious, directed mental activity rather than passive awareness of thought contents. When we think about something, it requires focused attention, intention, and cognitive processing abilities such as analysis, problem-solving, decision-making, memory recall, and envisioning possibilities. Some distinguishing characteristics of thinking processes include:

- They are proactive rather than reactive, guided by conscious goals or purposes rather than just conditions and conditioning.

- Thinking requires exerting mental effort, engagement, and intention rather than just letting thoughts arise automatically.

- It deals with abstract concepts, reasoning, evaluation, and imagination in a focused, linear manner versus scattered associative thinking.

- The same higher-order cognitive mechanisms are activated whether thinking about past, present, or hypothetical future scenarios.

- Language processing areas in the brain associated with explaining our thought process get involved.

On a cognitive level, thinking engages several brain networks working in concert, depending on the type of thinking required. Areas involved include the prefrontal cortex for reasoning and holding information temporarily online, the hippocampus for retrieving memories, sensory cortices for incorporating context, and so forth. Distinct networks even govern analytical vs. creative vs. social thinking modes.

While thoughts may informally occur during pauses in thinking, they largely happen independently in the background until brought to the forefront through focused thinking. Our greatest powers of problem-solving, decision-making, learning, and manifesting stem from taking charge of the thinking processes rather than just reacting to thoughts. With practice, we can shift into a mode of directing our thoughts purposefully and using them as tools for productive thinking.

Understanding the difference unlocks new ways to take charge of our mental processes for successful manifestation through directed, purposeful thinking over random thoughts beyond our control.

The Impact of Thoughts on Reality

Our thoughts have immense power in shaping our reality and experiences through the process of manifestation. Our habitual thought patterns influence our beliefs, perceptions, decisions, and ultimately the kind of life circumstances we attract on both subtle and material levels. Understanding this relationship sheds light on why we often find ourselves in situations corresponding to our internal outlook, even without always consciously intending it.

The Role of Belief Systems and Cognitive Biases

Underpinning our thoughts are fundamental belief systems formed from social conditioning and personal experiences that shape our assumptions about ourselves and the world. From childhood onward, beliefs become engrained cognitive filters that color how we interpret people and events. For example, someone abused as a child may develop beliefs like "People will hurt me" due to early experiences, subconsciously priming them to perceive neutral acts through a negative lens later on.

Closely related are cognitive biases—automatic mental shortcuts our brain relies on for efficient functioning that can skew thought processes without awareness if left unchecked. Common biases include confirmation bias, which involves selectively noticing details supporting views held, and negativity bias, which gives greater weight to potential threats versus opportunities. These inbuilt thinking patterns influence what conclusions we draw from ambiguous information and challenges.

Our dominant belief systems, combined with cognitive biases, work like self-fulfilling prophecies. They filter thoughts into awareness, promoting those aligning with the views held and suppressing alternatives. This means we unwittingly focus attention on evidence confirming beliefs while overlooking counter-evidence. For example, someone with beliefs around being unlucky will mentally spotlight stories verifying it rather than luck that comes their way too.

Relationship Between Thoughts and Manifestation

Turning to the role of individual thoughts, each one builds upon preceding thoughts to collectively shape end results. Within belief constructs, thoughts train the brain's synaptic structure through pattern recognition into similar rumination loops over time, reinforcing outlooks. Simple, repetitive thoughts of scarcity or gratitude, for example, rewire neural pathways, prompting corresponding experiences to manifest externally through the law of attraction.

From a thought-creates-reality framework, the consistent inner dialogue, images, and assumptions we hold from moment to moment eventually get projected as material circumstances through a more subtle flux of energy exchanges with the life force around us. Our perceived world arises from and corresponds to how we internally frame it through the lens of dominant, collectively held thoughts over time.

On a day-to-day level, switching perspectives on even mundane matters through more empowering thoughts can slightly nudge outcomes. Practicing catching prevalent beliefs fueling thought patterns like being unloved or undeserving of prosperity helps us become conscious co-creators of change. With consistency over weeks or months, this cultivation redirects the flow of life toward more fulfilling directions better aligned with true potential. Our mind is a fertile garden, so plant seeds of mental liberation intentionally for rich harvests!

Thoughts provide lenses that bring some possibilities into greater focus while dimming others, exactly as lenses do physically. By gradually recognizing thought systems and cognitive influences and retraining our focus toward what empowers us, we gain more sovereignty over the conscious creation of personal realities according to our highest ideals. The ability to shape life through thought alone is truly magical!

The Role of Thinking Processes in Manifestation

Now that we understand that thoughts and thinking are distinct experiences, let's explore how applying different thinking processes impacts manifestation.

Cognitive Processes That Influence Manifestation

While thoughts may arise spontaneously, we have a choice over the mental lens through which they are filtered and responded to. This power of perspective directly influences outcomes by determining whether intrusive thoughts control reactions or remain neutrally observed without attachment.

Rumination

Rumination involves repetitive, passive thinking focused on problems, worries, regrets, or self-criticism rather than solutions. It maintains a mental fixation on negative storylines that reinforce themselves with each loop. Studies link rumination to unhealthy coping habits as well as poorer mental and physical well-being over time by sustaining mental fixation in challenging loops versus conscious redirection (The Recovery Village, 2023). During manifestation, excessive rumination on doubts, lack, or past failures can attract undesirable outcomes through energetic alignment with those patterns.

Analysis

Another important cognitive process in manifestation is analysis—the active examination of thoughts, experiences, or goals to derive meaning. While light analysis seeks understanding and growth, overthinking drains energy in obsessive mental churning about minute details without resolution. It suspends action and decision-making in endless back-and-forth loops of minutiae versus the big picture. Manifestors learn to avoid chronic overanalysis that stresses mental focus better spent elsewhere.

Interpretation

Interpretation plays a role too in the narrative we apply. Our first interpretation of events may not always be the only or most empowering one possible with an altered perspective. Some choose to calmly reframe challenges in a learning-focused, solution-oriented light that elevates mood and opens new avenues rather than dwelling in perceived victimhood, expecting the worst, or blaming external luck. Such mindsets invigorate manifestation momentum.

Mindful Thinking to Support Manifestation

To cultivate mindful thinking conducive to goals, we can schedule periods for light contemplation amid busy lives. Clearing superficial thoughts allows core issues, truths, or potentials to surface naturally from our inner source of wisdom. This taps inspiration, steering daily actions and interactions fruitfully. Journaling sheds light on habitual thought patterns too by providing distance for observation without judgment, helping to consciously reshape mental defaults over time.

When manifesting, applying mindfulness helps notice thinking drifts into unconstructive loops and redirects inward peacefully without self-criticism. This mental self-regulation maintains present-moment focus, empowering choices versus entangling thoughts beyond control. We can add an anchor—a positive sentence, a mantra, or a word that makes us believe in the good—to mindfulness. Such purposeful thinking nourishes potent, coherent intentions that drive manifestation aligned with higher ambitions rather than leftover conditioning. With practice, new cognitive habits support continuous growth and fulfillment.

In any moment, we can take a deep breath and consciously adjust our thinking framework for improved manifestation results. Even small perspective shifts in how we interpret fleeting thoughts ripple outward into sustaining better realities. Making mindfulness a lifestyle integrates this finely-tuned interpretive control as second nature. Our minds are gardens; sow purposeful thinking seeds daily for an abundant, meaning-rich harvest.

Awareness of Thought Patterns

Our minds produce thousands of thoughts each day, many of which happen below our awareness. But to gain mastery over manifestation, it's important to foster mindfulness of habitual thought patterns we may not realize are holding us back. Mindfulness means paying attention purposefully in the present moment without judgment of what arises. When used to observe thoughts, it frees us from their hold, so new options can emerge.

Watching the Thinker

One mindfulness exercise for noticing thoughts is "watching the thinker," where we observe our mind in action yet remain an impartial witness rather than fully believing or identifying with thoughts. Imagine yourself on a meditation garden stroll, calmly noticing butterflies of mental chatter without reacting. This detachment creates valuable space for a wiser perspective on patterns potentially distorting reality.

Thought Labelling

Another is the "thought labeling" method. When a thought enters awareness, silently note its categories, such as worry, memory, or judgment—like labeling sights on a nature hike. The act of naming thought types trains focus away from attachment to contents. Journaling thoughts afterward without criticism reveals dynamics warranting more scrutiny, empowering proactive adjustments.

Once familiar with consistent thought themes through mindfulness, identify any keeping regular company. Common culprits creating suffering include repetitive worries about health, finances, or relationships fueled by vulnerability rather than fact. Another common pattern involves rigid thinking in terms of absolutist "shoulds" and "shouldn'ts" rather than openness.

Becoming aware of repetitive thought sequences opens doorways to conscious changes. Some find certain influences provoke worry spirals that foster a lack of mentality, harming goals. Small daily mindfulness shifts like closing news apps prone to bad news or limiting time dwelling negatively affect mental habits powerfully over weeks. We cultivate presence amid challenges through techniques of attending compassionately yet nonreactively to internal events.

Exercises like keeping a weekly thought journal help objectively spot thought themes, whether optimistic or negative. Note the circumstances surrounding patterns for insight into automatic triggers warranting new responses. Another helps reframe thoughts, catching yourself mid-worry spiral with questions like "How else could I interpret this?" Mindful breathing during both practices soothes the mind for a clearer perspective.

Through daily mindfulness of our internal dialogue, we lift veils on thought routines dictating realities. With compassion, this self-awareness releases old constraints, rewriting potential according to our highest good. Our thoughts chart life's course, so steer mindfulness there often for beautifully unfolding outcomes.

Aligning Thoughts and Actions

We've discussed how focused thought patterns influence manifestation, but true change happens when thinking meets tangible action. Unfortunately, our thoughts and behaviors don't always match up perfectly due to mental habits, self-doubt, or a lack of direction. However, aligning intentions and actions through congruence empowers thoughts by giving them life force to externally manifest quickly.

Incongruence stems from deeper thought processes, like ruminating on problems without solutions. We have empowering thoughts but cannot break cyclical patterns attached to past suffering. Or maybe believing "I can achieve my goal" yet procrastinating opportunities through limiting thought distortions. This disconnect dampens manifestation force since energy remains trapped conceptually versus expressed for results.

Journaling

The good news? With intention, we can synchronize thoughts to actions through strategic techniques that pull latent dreams from the mental to the physical realm by empowering doubts we once accepted. It starts with shedding light on triggers keeping inertia despite good intentions through thought journaling. Record experiences tugging you off-course, aside from empowering quotes challenging that narrative. Over time, patterns emerge, cueing new responses.

Micro-Tasking

Another strategy identifies minor, accessible steps toward wishes that seem too grand to seem alone, making achievement feel participatory versus fate-dependent. Deconstructing dreams into concrete actions scratches the itch for fulfillment, building habitual paths to bigger ends. Celebrate each accomplishment to reinforce congruence through positive reinforcement.

Visualization

Visualization also cements intention-action loops. Include sensory details such as enacting plans through willing embodiment, not detachment. Engage this active imagination daily, incorporating new scenarios of triumphs seamlessly into reality. Such mental rehearsal upgrades our brain wiring, attracting cooperative conditions through synced vibrational offering and reception.

Accountability

Accountability ensures action follows insights. Share reachable goals with supportive circles, inspiring responsibility through compassion.

Their presence strengthens will over inner resistance, tempted to revert from difficulty. Affirmation of efforts by others we respect sustains motivation to persevere where, alone, we may concede.

Mindfulness Meditation

Mindfulness Meditation calms judgmental thoughts, shielding our light. As inner chaos dissipates into stillness, we witness thought distortions for what they are—mental habits, not truth. With perspective, their hold dissolves, revealing courage transcending what once-limited beliefs about capable beings. This cultivation nourishes decisive, congruent choices based on wisdom versus worry alone.

By consciously closing the gap between intention and demonstration, we channel manifestation into purposeful flow, fulfilling destinies rather than passive daydreams. Integrating mind-body wisdom transforms wishes into concrete acts, aligning us magnetically to life's juiciest opportunities perfectly timed ahead. Our congruent offerings ripple outward from full hearts toward fellow travelers, elevating all.

Enhancing Badass Mindfulness

Transforming goals into reality requires synergy between focus and presence. Mindfulness cultivates exactly that: a calm, nonreactive frame, allowing empowered thought to flow unobstructed as manifest destiny. By maintaining detached yet engaged participation amid each moment's unfolding scenery within and out, we enrich manifestation through self-knowing alignment in action.

When desires rule awareness, yet thoughts race chaotically, manifestation momentum stalls without mindful guidance. But when combined, mindfulness nourishes concentrated intention, flowering outward. It starts by witnessing mental contents without attachment through breathing meditation. By not believing each thought as a fully formed personal truth, rumination loosens control for the open flow of new potentials.

This frees bandwidth by focusing single-pointedly on wishes during daily periods, versus defensiveness, which rigidifies around usual limits. One who sees thoughts objectively witnesses storylines for what they are—mental movies produced unconsciously like daydreams. With such separation, manifestation becomes proactive participation versus passive reception of what the mind imagines in isolation.

Once disidentification begins, practicing gratitude for life's intricacies anchors presence amid changing scenery within too. Noting beauty wherever it hides cultivates magnetic joy, uplifting all. This mindfulness strengthens intention, attracting collaborative people and opportunities smoothly falling into place through a cheerful outlook radiating fulfillment pre-arrival. Vision then springs effortlessly to three dimensions via small, aligned deeds, appreciating each step.

Integrating mindfulness everywhere transforms mundane tasks into meditation. While brushing your teeth, notice the texture and taste. During the commute, appreciate light entering slowly moving surroundings. Each mindful instant infuses ordinary acts with sacred essence, calming mental busyness and aligning physical deeds with grander visions, catalyzing manifestation. Days blend seamlessly into an effortlessly uplifting flow as mundane and marvelous intermingle through observant participation in all.

Additional mindfulness strategies include focused breathing during intentions to anchor present thinking. Imagery enhances intention by including rich sensory details. Keeping a daily journal trains objective observation by noting thought patterns for insight into habitual resistances and happier alternatives. Accountability through sharing goals supports ongoing manifestation through relationships without judgment or fixation on results alone.

Each mindful moment creates space, allowing more of life's hidden beauty and opportunities to enter the conscious experience. So, fill pauses consciously through breathing, nature connection, or creativity instead of automatic distraction, providing an unhealthy escape from presence. Make sitting meditation a priority whenever tension arises, tightening thoughts from stress or unrest, soothing the mind back to calm waters, and manifesting wishes as a natural result.

With mindfulness, all life participates in co-creation rather than reacting to imagined limits alone. Our highest nature emerges through peaceful yet proactive engagement everywhere as a single-minded yet spacious, flowing presence. In this flow, manifestation happens as a happy surprise versus an end destination alone, becoming joyful participation that uplifts all. May your mindfulness multiply life's gifts endlessly!

Chapter 4:

Badass Mindfulness Techniques

Badass Mindfulness is the art of manifesting by applying focused awareness and presence of mind to your goals and visualizations. It is about being fully conscious and attentive to every thought, feeling, action, and experience related to what you want to create in your life. The key is not just thinking and dreaming about your desires but also skillfully directing your mind, body, and energy in a way that aligns your inner and outer worlds.

This chapter is dedicated to sharing simple yet highly effective techniques that you can start practicing right away to consciously manifest positive changes in a mindful manner. These techniques have been used by masters of manifestation throughout history to materialize incredible realities from nothing but a seed of intention. With practice, they can also help you experience transformative results.

Let us start with daily visualization. Your thoughts shape your reality, so see your desires as already fulfilled by forming vivid mental images every day. Picture the fulfillment of your goals as clearly as possible, using all your senses. Give your visualization energy and emotion. See yourself experiencing joy in attainment. Make visualization a habit for at least 15 minutes a day to saturate your subconscious with images of what you want. This will guide your mindful actions and attract opportunities.

Another crucial technique is journaling. Once visualized, your goals need manifestation fuel in the form of clear intentions, beliefs, and feelings. Journal daily to document your detailed intentions, express deep gratitude for what you want as if you already have it, and pour out positive emotions. Read your journal before sleep and first thing in the morning to remind your subconscious of your powerful intentions. This will program your mind to work in alignment with your goals.

Meditation is the foundation for mindful badass mindfulness. Even five minutes daily of focusing on deep breathing helps calm the analytical mind and invokes a receptive state where you become a clear channel for the conscious creation of your reality. Meditate regularly to cultivate the presence of mind which will help optimize visualization and manifestation actions intuitively guided from within.

Speaking and writing affirmations out loud are extremely powerful. Saying affirmations programs your subconscious with messages of fulfillment at a deeper level than just thinking about them. Out loud affirmations engrain the feeling of already having what you want. Affirm your goals as facts in the present tense daily, such as "I am so grateful and happy now that I have manifested true love." Repeat daily affirmations throughout the day for the best results.

Surround yourself with reminders of what you desire, such as posters, saved pictures on your phone, and quotes or affirmations written around the house, to constantly internalize what you want to attract. Listen daily to subliminal manifestation tracks or positive audios that can seep into your subconscious mind. Wear, carry, or surround yourself with anything tactile as a physical representation of your goals. Staying constantly immersed in the visualization and feeling of already having what you want is key to consciously manifesting it.

Gratitude is a powerhouse technique. Shift your mindset to feel grateful for what you do have right now instead of emphasizing lack. Be thankful for the things and people that helped you get closer to your goal, even if indirectly. Gratitude opens you up to the receptivity of more blessings. Make a daily note of three things that you are grateful for related to your intentions to keep the energy of gratitude flowing.

Act as if you are already manifesting what you want by adopting the behaviors, mannerisms, and attitudes of having fulfilled your goals. If you want a new home, for example, search for photos of dream homes online while filled with joy instead of wishing. If you desire a loving marriage, start nurturing small ways to express care for those around you now. Taking mindful action based on the present feeling of fulfillment helps make it a self-fulfilling prophecy.

Once you mindfully align your inner and outer worlds, doors will magically open, providing opportunities and resources and helping to turn your desires into realities. Look for meaningful coincidences and be ready to seize them. But do not just wait for signs passively. Signal what you want actively through the techniques of mindful present-moment awareness to attract an aligned flow of circumstances. This prepares your optimal state to materialize your dreams.

While intentions precede manifestation, it is the skillful application of techniques like visualization, journaling, meditation, affirmations, gratitude, acting as if, and attracting synchronicity that allows you to consciously steer your dominant thoughts and consciously direct your mindful actions according to your desired outcome. With regular practice of mindfulness in manifestation, you will shift from passively wishing to actively attracting your heart's desires effortlessly. If you apply at least a few of these badass mindfulness techniques consistently in your daily life, you will experience accelerated results.

Mental Rehearsal

Mental rehearsal is a powerful manifestation technique that involves envisioning your goals as if they are already a reality. Let's start by understanding what exactly mental rehearsal is and its significance in the process of conscious creation.

Mental rehearsal means vividly imagining the fulfillment of your desires, using as many sensory details as you can. It's like a mental simulation where you see, feel, hear, and experience having already manifested what you want. You envision taking actions, and having conversations associated with your goals being achieved. Mental rehearsal trains your subconscious mind to think and feel as if your desires are now present. It programs your beliefs at a deeper level.

The Role of Mental Rehearsal in Manifestation

Our thoughts become things. Repeated mental imagery of any scenario embeds it deeply in your mind until it manifests physically through your aligned actions. Mental rehearsal of outcomes makes them feel true, building expectation and intention. This primed state allows you to naturally take mindful steps to attract circumstances supporting your goals. Regularly envisioning goals as facts programs your dominant thoughts and subconscious to believe and behave consistent with fulfillment already being real. Mental rehearsal plays a pivotal role in consciously steering manifestation.

A Step-by-Step Guide to Mental Rehearsal Practices

Set aside 10–15 minutes daily in a quiet place with no distractions. Relax your body and breathe deeply to invoke a calm, focused, and receptive state of mind. Visualize your goals in the present tense from a first-person perspective:

- See yourself experiencing the fulfillment of your desires in vivid, sensory-rich detail, as if it's actually occurring. Look around, noticing sights, sounds, smells, and textures.

- Feel genuine happiness and gratitude arising from attaining your dreams. Immerse yourself in the positive emotions surrounding fulfillment.

- Pay attention to the thoughts, conversations, and actions associated with the realization of your goals. Hear yourself discussing achievement with others joyfully.

- Involve all your senses to make the experience as realistic as possible. Hear congratulatory voices, feel the textures of attained objects, and smell scents symbolic of materialization.

- Envision roadblocks dissolving and support rising to help you reach your destination with ease and delight.

- Savor the simulation for its entire duration without critical thought. Believe it's happening presently.

- Repeat the visualization daily at the same time for powerful programming effects to emerge over weeks.

- Feel free to modify scenarios based on intuitive guidance. Add or remove details to maintain vividness and enthusiasm.

- Journal about your experience immediately after to reinforce it mentally. Note synchronicities.

Amplify manifestation momentum by telling a trusted person about your experience of fulfillment. Rehearse conversations as if goals have already been achieved to further embed the desired reality through additional senses of hearing and speaking.

When I was a teenager, I really wanted my own horse to ride. One day, a friend was telling me all about the fun times she had riding a horse with someone she knew. I had been hoping for a similar chance but wasn't finding the right connection. In that moment, I told her I had a horse too and could go riding alone sometimes. Of course, that wasn't true; I just really wanted it to be. But soon after, my mom's friend offered to let me help care for her horse. She trusted that I could ride alone, and I took great care of the animal. Looking back, I did manifest what I wanted strongly by imagining with all my senses that it was true in the moment.

Mentally relieve visualized success anytime and anywhere thoughts stray from fulfillment. Redirecting pervasive mental imagery is key.

Be on the lookout for magical open doors and opportunities aligning circumstances with your heartfelt intention. Mental rehearsal primes you to recognize and actualize opportunities. Stay alert yet relaxed.

With regular mental rehearsal practice, your subconscious programming shifts to truly believing and expecting, having already manifested your focused desires. Beliefs drive the manifestation engine. Mental rehearsal supercharges your conscious ability to draw goals into reality through skillful belief embedding at a micro level every day until magic is made routine.

So, in essence, mental rehearsal is a potent technique where envisioning with details activates the limitless manifestation abilities within you. Using all senses to vividly simulate fulfillment primes your mind and energy to align with actual materialization in a natural flow. With persistent practice, mental rehearsal elevates your manifestation skills from possible to probable to inevitable!

Energy Alignment Exercises

Our reality is shaped by the energetic vibrational frequency of our thoughts and emotions. Understanding energy is essential to consciously manifesting your highest dreams. Let's explore the concepts of energy and vibration, along with practical exercises to raise your manifestation frequency.

Understanding Energy and Vibration

Everything in the universe, seen or unseen, is made of energy, which can be at different vibrational speeds. Energy gives form to matter and drives transformation. Our bodies, too, are highly energetic beings responding to the environment through electric and magnetic energies in atoms and molecules. Thoughts and feelings emit unique vibrations decoded by our subconscious to match our outer world. This gives us power over co-creating circumstances by controlling inner vibrations.

The Concept of Vibration and Frequency

The higher the frequency of vibration, the higher the level of manifestation. Where attention goes, energy flows. Focused thinking and emotions emit electromagnetic pulses of precise frequencies decoded by the field of infinite possibilities. Lower vibrations match lack and limitation, while higher ones attract joy, ease, and abundance.

To manifest consciously, one must raise inner vibrational set points from old self-sabotaging patterns. This upgrades our personal frequency to align with fulfillment, which has to materialize out of energetic compatibility rather than willpower. Hence, practicing energy awareness and alignment is crucial for badass mindfulness.

Energy Alignment Techniques

Meditation is an exceptionally beneficial practice to refine our conscious vibration. Practicing diaphragm breathing (belly breathing) by inhaling and exhaling while focusing on breath empties mental clutter and helps perceive subtle energetic sensations within. It invokes a receptive alpha state conducive to creative manifestation work.

Belly Breathing

Start by sitting comfortably, keeping the spine straight yet relaxed. Soften the gaze while bringing attention to natural breathing without controlling it. Gentle inhales energize, while exhales release tension. Note thoughts without judgment and softly bring focus back to breath. Repeat a soothing mantra or affirmation if your mind wanders. Stay present for at least 7–15 minutes daily for the best results. Meditation is a powerful way to consciously raise energetic frequencies and optimize manifestation.

Breathwork

Breathwork is another deeply transformative exercise for inner alignment. There are many pranayama (yogic breathing techniques), but a simple one is abdominal breathing. Place one palm on the belly and the other on the chest. Inhale through the nose, feeling the belly expand; exhale through the nose, feeling your lungs emptying. While inhaling, imagine light coming into your body. Hold your breath for 2–3 seconds, imaging the light in all of your body, then exhale and let go of everything. Just relax until you feel ready to take the next inhale. Start with five rounds, increasing to ten over the next few weeks. Deep-focused breathing stimulates the vagus nerve, which regulates stress, and pulls us into a receptive state where we can consciously embody higher frequencies.

Grounding

Grounding is essential for energy coherence and manifestation flow. Find comfortable seated or standing positions with feet flat on the earth and palms down. Visualize roots extending from your pelvic floor and soles into the earth's electromagnetic field. Feel your energy centers aligning as earth energy flows up through chakras and our crown. Grounding dissipates overwhelm and centers us energetically for empowered manifestation. Studies show grounding reduces inflammation (Oschman et al., 2015). Repeat for 5–10 minutes.

Energy Clearing and Protection

Energy clearing and protection are helpful to shed limiting beliefs that block fulfillment. Start by envisioning purifying white light filling and radiating out every cell of your being. See or sense any darkness or clutter releasing effortlessly through the light's blessing. Affirm protection from unhealthy intrusions daily, and visualize yourself wrapped in a glowing white forcefield. These energy practices uplift your radiance and aura for manifestational magic.

These alignment techniques form a holistic, energetic foundation for realizing your dreams. Through dedicated daily practice, you will raise your vibration to coherence with higher outcomes. While consciously attracting desired circumstances, stay vigilant not to drop frequency through disempowering thoughts. Uplift yourself and others to embody a manifestation mastery frequency and experience magic!

Symbols and Rituals for Manifestation

Manifestation relies heavily on thought and emotion energy—the power of focused intention. Incorporating meaningful symbols and rituals fuels this manifesting mojo.

The Role of Symbols and Rituals in Manifestation

Symbols and rituals tap into deeper creative patterns and spiritual beliefs through symbols that represent ideas. Engaging visuals, tactiles, and routines anchor conscious desires, activating subconscious programming. Well-crafted rituals frame manifestation as a devout practice, uplifting expectations beyond temporary motivations. Regular symbolic acts cultivate receptivity to opportunities that fulfill focused intentions. An aligned daily manifestation practice centered on personal symbols and rituals amplifies the energetic drive for materialization.

The Significance of Personalizing Symbols and Rituals

Off-the-shelf manifestation methods lack resonance and lack tailored spirituality. Select items imbued with personal significance as visual symbols of your goals. For example, if you want a new home, frame a housewarming card as an altar centerpiece. Tie a ribbon around a tree if you want a new relationship. Get creative in designing artifacts that embody desires while invoking delight at their future arrival.

Similarly, craft rituals around personally meaningful routines; for instance, lighting incense while journaling while prepping morning coffee infuses sacredness into daily tasks. Over time, these symbols and rituals become pathways to the numinous, attracting magic. Associating desires with enjoyable symbolic acts naturally elevates expectancy, aiding manifestation flow.

Examples of Cultural Symbols and Rituals

Ritual candle lighting is commonly used in Latin American traditions to manifest purposes while burning intention papers as offerings. Some place items desired under the full moon to harness its fertile vibes.

In Asian cultures, feng shui principles utilize symbolic arrangements and directions based on elements signifying abundance, career, relationships, and so on. Colors also convey nuanced meanings for manifestation.

In Native American ceremonies, sacred pipes filled with tobacco requests are smoked, circulating prayers skyward. Feathers, stones, crystals, and totems possess symbolic attributes supporting focused manifestation work too.

Islamic scriptures reference reciting surahs and verses as manifestation rituals believed to connect petitioners directly with divine assistance. Symbolic zikr bead counting, or dhikr remembrance, is also a potent way to infuse presence when invoking desires.

Africans place wishes in ritual river, lake, or sea offerings, believing ancients accepted gifts carrying intentions to fruition. Drumming, dancing, and costumes too hold deep symbolic energy, transferring focused intent's momentum for fulfillment.

Celtic and Wiccan traditions use cauldrons filled with symbolic tokens like roses and crystals for moonlit blessings upon intentions. Visualizations accompanied by selected meaningful herbs, colors, candles, and rituals weave intent from imagination to reality.

Creative ritual elements need not belong to specific cultures or faiths. Adopt ideas respecting original contexts to craft personalized manifestation systems blended with varied symbolic inspirations. With dedicated symbolic ritual practice and patience, goals are energetically catalyzed into concrete realities.

Meaning-making through symbols and ritual cultivates a felt sense, anchoring intention as already existing beyond thoughts. This primes manifestation readiness, attracting fulfillment through behavioral resonance with focused items and routines. Explore elements sparking personal resonance for turbocharging conscious creation goals through potent symbolic ritual amplification. Your unique sacred aspirations and focused symbols hold the keys to opening manifestation doors!

Vision Board Creation

Vision boards are a fun, creative way to energize your dreams into physical form. Simply put, a vision board is a collage that visually represents your goals, desires, and intentions. This tool serves to charge your manifestation powers through powerful visualization.

The Concept of Vision Boards

A vision board collects inspiring pictures and words that center your focus on what you want to experience in life. It's a snapshot of your envisioned future. As you craft and engage with your board daily, you broadcast a vibrational signal, drawing those intentions into reality through the law of resonance. Your mind is filled with positive images, aligning subconscious programming to expect fulfillment.

Choosing Images and Words

Carefully select images and words that reflect your deepest heart's desires. Browse magazines, and photos online, or cut out pictures you connect to on a soul level. Choose items that activate feelings of accomplishment, joy, and gratitude related to each intention. Include images that stimulate your senses, like destination travel boards depicting scenic photos. Add affirming words, amount figures, and dates representing your goals too.

Laying Out Your Board

Use a natural material like cardboard, cork, or poster board as your canvas. Arrange images and words in an appealing, energetic layout that uplifts your mood. Leave some whitespace for future inspiration. Use embellishments that spark your creativity—ribbons, markers, stickers, scrapbooking paper. You can make multiple themed boards for different areas. Sign and date your board as a true expression of yourself.

Engaging with Your Vision Board Daily

View your board first thing in the morning and last thing at night for at least 5–10 minutes as bookends, infusing your day's energy with visualized success. Focus on feeling fulfilled by each item while observing the bigger picture of your new reality and noticing new details emerge over time. Your board program attitudes, unlocking opportunities, appear miraculous. Have faith—the magic works!

Updating and Expanding Your Vision

Revisit your board periodically, adding or removing items, to maintain enthusiasm. Cut out new inspirations that surface, reflecting evolving goals or synchronous notices. Freshen images that lose vivacity from overexposure. Expand categories on yearly anniversary boards, tracking progress and adjusted intentions. Use markers to code items manifested to revel in triumphs while adjusting visualizations for upcoming cycles.

Turn Your Vision Board Into an Affirmation Tool

Weekly or monthly, speak aloud about positive outcomes represented in photos while gazing intently at clustered intentions on your board. Feel belief-building with each detail-filled statement. You can journal responses, ideas, and synchronicities that arise too. Audible affirmations cement fulfilled realities deep within your subconscious mind.

Your vision board is a potent companion, fueling your badass mindfulness practice. I use my vision board for the affirmations. Every morning, I read aloud the affirmations that are written on my vision board, which is placed next to a mirror. This greatly aided me in accomplishing my goals. By thoughtfully selecting images and engaging your board regularly, you charge your desires with a focused energy of fulfillment. With faith in the law of attraction and yourself, dream big—your customized vision board holds the manifesting keys to transforming incredible life visions into happy realities. Your future is yours to consciously create!

Rituals for Release and Surrender

Manifesting can sometimes feel like an uphill battle as we struggle to detach from preconceived notions of how fulfillment should appear. However, an essential piece of consciously creating is embracing flexibility through releasing resistance and surrendering desired outcomes. Allowing space for magic without attachment invites synchronicity to work naturally. Rituals centered on release and surrender optimize manifestation flow.

The Importance of Release and Surrender in Manifestation

When we tightly grip outcomes mentally, that very tension undermines manifestation momentum. Clinging to how or when goals materialize breeds stress, limiting frequency alignment for fulfillment. Surrendering attached stakes fosters receptiveness toward divine timing beyond human control. This relinquishes overwhelm, empowering faith that desires manifest in unexpected perfection.

Release rituals purge emotions, blocking intended realities. Letting go of resentments, regret, or fear through ceremony liberates us from energetic congestion and stagnating manifestation currents. Such practices optimize vibration coherence, which is essential to consciously drawing goals. Surrender accepts what is with serenity, cultivating presence integral to perceiving subtle clues and aiding destiny's natural unfolding.

Rituals for Releasing Resistance

Write desires needing release on strips of paper. Visualize intentions dissolving, then burn them, invoking transformation through fire's symbolism. Scatter ashes, wishing well for former limitations' ends while appreciating life's lessons.

Another release ritual involves submerging intentions' papers in a body of moving water like a creek or ocean, allowing natural currents to carry away stagnant vibrations. Feel uplifted afterward by this symbolic cleansing.

Releasing can also involve speaking affirmations, dissolving resistance, and smudging yourself and your home with cleansing plants like sage, sweetgrass, or incense to purify habitual resistance patterning on mental-emotional levels. Repeat as guided intuitively.

Rituals for Surrendering Outcomes

Write goals you feel attached to the timing or form of on paper, then bury them in Mother Earth's patient womb, trusting divine timing beyond rational understanding or control. Tend the spot with daily prayers, appreciating life's sacred unfolding however it arises. Your role is your intention alone.

Another surrender ritual holds releasing intentions written on leaves, which are respectfully offered to the currents of a moving creek or sea, symbolizing faith that your desires flow where needed when ripened. Let go of anticipating how the magic happens and settle into present peace instead.

Light a ceremonial yellow or white candle daily, dedicating its steady burning to your practice of surrendering outcomes peacefully to spirit. Affirm the release of all stakes in premeditated results while accepting life's mysteries with grace and gratitude. Calmly extinguish the flame when it is complete.

Incorporating Release and Surrender in Practice

Begin manifestation rituals by stating your intention, then reciting affirmations incorporating phrases like "I release resistance" or "I trust perfect timing." Smudge yourself and your envisioned goals following affirmations to purge attachment.

Burn slips list formerly resistant thoughts and emotions after energizing desires, symbolic of release aiding cultivation. Tend a sacred surrender tree or plant by your home, infusing daily intentions with flexibility.

Journal any resistance surrounding desires and read affirming reminders dissolving each concern. Shred entries when released, and install acceptance as your new foundation for receiving fulfillment; however, it ripens in divine order.

Rituals cultivating release and surrender optimize our energetic flow, attracting opportunities beyond human limitation. Trust the unseen tide carrying your dreams precisely as destined. Magic favors those with faith in possibility over specific results. Surrender brings true peace, enabling conscious creation's fullest blessings.

Chapter 5:

Embracing Vulnerability in

Manifestation

For a long time, many of us have believed that to be successful in manifesting our desires, we need to appear strong, confident, and in control at all times. We think showing any sign of weakness or vulnerability will destroy our chances of getting what we want. While confidence is important, true manifestation depends much more on our willingness to embrace vulnerability. By embracing our vulnerability, paradoxically, we give ourselves the best opportunity to manifest successfully.

What exactly do I mean by vulnerability? Simply put, vulnerability means being willing to show up as we really are—both our strengths and weaknesses, both the feelings we're comfortable with and those that scare us. It means letting others see that imperfection is our nature as humans. We all have moments of self-doubt, fear, uncertainty, and a lack of confidence. Vulnerability means acknowledging those moments in ourselves and communicating them to others when appropriate, instead of pretending we have it all together. It means not censoring how we truly feel inside out of a belief that we won't be liked or respected if we share our imperfect humanity.

Living vulnerably might seem terrifying if we think it means falling apart emotionally or losing our dignity. But real vulnerability is actually a sign of emotional and mental strength. It takes courage to acknowledge our weaknesses and embrace the whole of who we are— light and dark, joyful and afraid. When we're willing to show our soft underbelly, it allows others to connect with us through empathy rather than keeping them at a distance by always appearing invincible.

Vulnerability fosters authentic connections between people by facilitating honest, meaningful communication.

So, why is vulnerability important for manifestation success? The reason is that authenticity is key for aligning our inner and outer selves. Our inner thoughts and feelings fuel the vibration that either helps or hinders our manifestations. When we deny or repress weaknesses to seem strong, we introduce internal disharmony that interferes with the natural flow of energy. Inner misalignment makes it much harder for the external world to resonate with our intentions. But vulnerability creates alignment. By embracing all of who we are inside through self-acceptance, our inner and outer selves sing in harmony, which opens channels for co-creative energy to work through us with ease.

Vulnerability also builds trust between ourselves and the divine power that grants our manifestations. If we're unwilling to show what we see as flaws, how can we truly let go and allow the flow of receiving from a benevolent higher force? Keeping parts of ourselves guarded communicates a lack of trust. But vulnerability exercises faith that we'll be supported through both joy and pain. It grants permission for life's ebb and flow in a spirit of open-handedness rather than resistance. With that attitude of trust, manifestations come more easily as we let divine orchestration work its magic.

Opening to vulnerability takes practice because trying to always maintain an image of perfect strength and control is such a conditioned habit. But with experience, we find that showing weakness doesn't diminish our worth; instead, it adds depth and humanity that others find relatable and likable. Take a customer service representative, for instance. If they smile through obvious stress over an impossible workload, we resent being fake-smiled at. But if they admit they're feeling overwhelmed, most customers will be encouraged to extend patience and compassion. Authenticity invites support. Meanwhile, someone who appears constantly composed may come across as aloof or artificially superior rather than like the real person we'd want to connect with.

A key part of vulnerability is openly discussing our manifestations—not just successes but also perceived failures and setbacks. Those times when things aren't going as planned are often the most instructive for learning how to improve our processes. But we tend to hide difficulties, believing they stigmatize us as less capable. This leaves us isolated from facing challenges and unable to benefit from others' potential insights. Openly communicating vulnerability builds comradery and support systems to encourage positive mindsets through making fun of yourself. Not taking yourself too seriously and making fun of a really scary situation. This is the part of letting go and accepting a situation or feeling you are in. And those who are struggling too can feel less alone. Manifestation, like life itself, is a process with ebbs and flows. By embracing vulnerability through transparency, failure loses its power to discourage us from continuing our creative journey.

So, shedding the skin of an image-conscious "perfect manifestor" allows our authentic energy to flow freely and aligns us with supportive divine forces and community connections. Practice vulnerability by communicating even uncomfortable feelings with care, trusting the process, and showing up for yourself and others with compassion. Make of your whole self—strengths and weaknesses—an offering of faith that what you truly need will find you in good time. When we embrace vulnerability, it paradoxically unleashes our greatest potential for manifestation success as we journey through life together.

Power of Vulnerability

Many of us see vulnerability as a weakness, something to avoid at all costs. But true strength isn't about always appearing strong; it's about having the courage to show up as we are, with all our flaws, doubts, and fears on display. Vulnerability plays a huge role in our personal growth, our relationships, and our ability to manifest what we want in life.

Vulnerability vs. Weakness

We must distinguish vulnerability from weakness. Being vulnerable doesn't mean falling apart or losing control of our emotions. It's simply showing all of who we are, including the parts we feel are imperfect. Real strength is having the guts to admit when we don't have it totally together and to let people see our softer side too. Strength isn't about never feeling vulnerable; it's about being vulnerable anyway, despite feeling afraid. True power lies in our willingness to acknowledge that perfection is impossible and accept all parts of ourselves with compassion.

Benefits

Many benefits come from embracing vulnerability. First, it aligns our inner and outer selves so our thoughts and feelings are flowing in harmony rather than fighting against each other. When we repress weaknesses or flaws, we introduce inner conflict that gets in the way of achieving our goals. But vulnerability creates inner alignment that opens channels for the natural flow of creative energy. It helps us manifest by reducing internal blockages to the free exchange of positive energy.

Second, vulnerability builds trust between ourselves and the divine, higher forces that grant our manifestations. If we hide parts of ourselves, we imply a lack of faith that we'll be unconditionally supported. But vulnerability exercises faith that we'll be okay even through hard times, which strengthens our energetic connection to guidance. Open-handedness about life's twists and turns fosters an attitude that makes manifestations happen more easily as we surrender control over outcomes.

Third, vulnerability allows honest, meaningful connections with others that are extremely important for manifestation support. No one can achieve big goals alone; we need support systems to encourage positive thinking, especially during low points. But we often isolate ourselves when we feel we're not measuring up. Vulnerability means accepting help graciously when we need it. It fosters empathy in relationships as people witness our humanness instead of seeing a flawless facade. This builds community strength around us to boost manifestation abilities.

Fourth, embracing vulnerability through transparency creates space for learning from both successes and perceived failures. Manifesting isn't linear; there are always problems to work out along the journey. Hiding struggles prevents gaining insights from others who've faced similar challenges. But openly communicating difficulties builds understanding and comradery to encourage positive mindsets even through tough times. No one feels alone in their process. And lessons from failures can teach us more than victories do.

Fifth, vulnerability paradoxically increases likability and connection with others. Being completely authentic invites others to feel comfortable sharing their own true selves, resulting in closer bonds built on understanding each person's whole experience—light and shadow. On the other hand, constantly appearing perfectly strong and controlled often creates a disconnect, making human encounters feel artificial.

In the end, vulnerability's power lies not in any single outcome but in how it fosters alignment, trust, honesty, and community—all fuel for successful manifestation. By seeing our humanness as beautiful rather than flawed and embracing each part with compassion, vulnerability becomes the doorway to our highest creative expression and well-being. It's a risk, but one that pays off tremendously in terms of personal evolution and manifestation. Courage belongs to those who are willing to feel afraid and vulnerable anyway.

Overcoming the Fear of Vulnerability

While vulnerability can yield great rewards, it often seems downright terrifying. Most of us have lingering fears about being vulnerable that hold us back from really connecting with others or achieving our potential.

Reasons

One major reason vulnerability scares us is that we worry about how others will judge or perceive us if we show weaknesses or imperfections. From a young age, we get the message that flaws make us unworthy of love, respect, or opportunity. But the truth is, people are far more empathetic than we assume—they too struggle just to get through each day. We all contain a beautiful mess of contradictions! While judgment may come, expressing your authentic self is far healthier than repressing parts to avoid disapproval that likely won't come anyway. You owe it to yourself to show up as is.

Fear of rejection also fuels vulnerability avoidance. Intimacy in relationships requires accepting that not connecting 100% of the time with 100% of people is normal and okay. Worrying constantly about what others think traps us in a box of social anxiety instead of living freely. With practice, it gets easier to let people's individual preferences say nothing about your inherent worth. You'll attract those meant to appreciate you as you are.

Lack of confidence in our abilities or ideas paralyzes us from putting ourselves out there too. But confidence comes from small acts of bravery over time, not mind-reading acceptance beforehand. Falling on your face is human; what matters most is getting back up with lessons learned so you can soar even higher next time. And you never know—what you bring to the table may be just what someone needs!

Another hurdle stems from believing we must stay in absolute control. But life involves imperfection and chaos beyond our abilities to perfectly direct. Focusing inwardly gives peace instead of stressing over external variables you can't change. When you let go of the pressure to always maintain composure, connection and creativity flow naturally.

Overcoming Fear of Vulnerability

Start small:

- Consciously share one authentic thought or feeling daily with someone you trust, like expressing a worry without solutions required.

- Listen without judgment when others open up to you to build trust; reciprocity is safe.

- Celebrate each tiny act of vulnerability as growing courage—not failure, if not perfectly brave.

- Write down perceived flaws you struggle to communicate and recite affirming mantras like, "I am enough."

- Join groups with like-minded souls to feel part of something bigger, supporting vulnerability journeys.

With practice over time, vulnerability fears lessen as you experience unconditional acceptance from within and without. Keep diving inward to identify blocks, then rise each day committed to consciously replacing resistances with radical self-love.

Remember, difficulty sharing all of who you are says nothing about your intrinsic worth. You deserve unreserved love for simply being alive. Have faith that by opening courageously to life's ups and downs, you make space for fulfillment, growth, and deep connection, which are the most fulfilling parts of the human experience. Your vulnerabilities are not faults to bury, but gifts meant to be shared.

The journey to brave vulnerability takes dedication. But each small act of honest, open-hearted living strengthens your determination to walk boldly in your truth. With patience and compassion for yourself, you'll come to see all parts of your experience as beautiful. And in that process lies freedom, creativity, and a life lived without fear of being wonderfully, messily human.

Vulnerability as a Gateway to Emotional Healing

While vulnerability seems frightening, it provides an important doorway to emotional healing. Unaddressed wounds from our past often resurface unconsciously, blocking the free flow of creative energies needed for manifestation. But facing difficulties vulnerably with courage and care sets the stage for inner transformations that uplift our lives immensely.

How Vulnerability Heals Emotional Wounds

Most of us carry deep emotional scars, big or small, arising from various hurtful experiences like abuse, loss, divorce, or childhood challenges. The natural response is to bury the pain deep to avoid re-feeling it. However, this creates walls between our conscious and subconscious minds. Walls introduce inner conflict, preventing clear manifestation focus. Our energy gets tied to addressing old wounds instead of creating new blessings.

Pain demands to be felt when it is ready to teach its lessons for personal evolution. So, though scary, vulnerability helps work through traumas by safely embracing difficult feelings and memories non-judgmentally as they arise. This integration process offers deep healing by making peace with past darkness and regaining inner power stolen by hurt. Alignment emerges as we accept all parts as belonging to us.

Still, opening vulnerabilities requires tender care, like coaxing a skittish animal to feel safe enough to come near. Start small through journaling, artwork, or kind, supportive communities. Honoring feelings without rushing resolution encourages sensitive healing at your natural pace. Impatience retraumatizes; compassion cultivates courage, facing fears as patiently as strength allows. Regular emotional release through tears, dance, or rituals eases repressed pain's hold over time.

The Connection Between Emotional Healing and Manifestation

Healing creates inner calm, aligning the subconscious with the desires of the conscious, creative mind. Clear channels then exist for manifestation energy to flow unburdened by past limitations. Where trauma once blocked success, healing opens unlimited potential realized through new experiences of life, love, and creative ventures freely pursued. We attract more fully based on healed truths about our worth instead of wounds mistaking us as unworthy.

Recognizing trauma's lesson and empowering us also lifts its power over present circumstances. What once seemed like obstacles we blamed ourselves for can be reframed as opportunities teaching mastery over life's challenges, now overcome through vulnerability's healing gifts. This shift transforms defeating self-talk and limiting new creations into upbeat affirmations of strength and hope. Emotions no longer control manifestation abilities but fuel them.

So, while vulnerability exposes raw places, its patient embrace administered with care, self-acceptance, and community yields emotional Phoenix-like rebirths. Healing connects all parts of oneself, severing the past from present-empowered outlooks. With walls and blockages gone, manifestation flows strongest yet gentle, guided by life's blessings matched to our deepest truths of divine, deserving wholeness. Courage to feel vulnerable wherever fear lingers grants spiritual liberation and its abundant manifestations.

Vulnerability in Practice

While vulnerability seems difficult, it can be developed through consistent practice. Regular application can make honest self-expression feel more natural over time.

Journaling

Journaling is extremely helpful for exploring vulnerable inner experiences. Set a timer for 10 minutes daily, and freely journal whatever comes to mind without editing yourself. Try prompts like:

- What am I feeling right now, and why?

- What flaws am I working on accepting about myself?

- What fears hold me back, and how can I build courage?

- What kinds of situations trigger me to close off, and how can I practice openness instead?

Simply getting thoughts out of your head and onto paper through uncensored writing is liberating. You don't need to show anyone; it's for your own growth.

Mindful Meditation

Mindfulness meditation also aids vulnerability by encouraging non-judgmental presence. Spend five minutes focusing solely on your breath without distractions to center inward. Notice passing thoughts and return focus gently to breathing whenever the mind wanders. At the end, reflect vulnerably on your experience. What did this session reveal about how judgment encroaches on simply being present? With practice, you'll get better at observing yourself non-critically.

Progressive Muscle Relaxation

Progressive muscle relaxation can help physically release vulnerability barriers. Tense and relax each major muscle group slowly while breathing deeply. Pay attention to any tension you're unconsciously holding and breathe into relaxing those areas fully. At the end, observe how stress manifests physically and how relaxation feels; this builds awareness around vulnerability triggers.

Gratitude

Gratitude practices like daily listing things you appreciate cultivate vulnerability by shifting perspective from flaws to assets or blessings. It also fosters community by sharing your list with others to appreciate each other mutually.

Sharing

Sharing with trusted people aids vulnerability. Start small—share one genuine thought, feeling, or experience that's hard to express but won't damage you if received poorly. Listen without fixing when others share vulnerably to build mutual understanding.

Test experiential vulnerability by doing one stimulating new activity weekly where you may feel silly, like an art class, hiking, or comedy night. Notice judgments that arise and replace them with compassion for wherever you're in the learning process. Growth happens outside of comfort zones.

Vulnerability takes daring, but also kindness toward yourself. Commit to these practices regularly while expressing self-care and patience if progress feels slow. Celebrate every small act of brave living; you're worthy as you discover and share your whole, beautiful self. With effort over time, courageous vulnerability transforms from intimidating to second nature.

Gratitude Journaling

Being grateful for what we have is important for manifestation. It keeps us focusing on possibilities instead of limits and fosters receptivity to new blessings. One powerful yet simple practice is gratitude journaling—taking just a few minutes daily to record things we appreciate. Regular journaling has been shown to improve mood, health, and relationships (Bailey, 2018). It also develops vulnerability in ways that aid the creative manifestation process.

When we're vulnerable, by acknowledging both strengths and shortcomings openly, inner and outer alignment results. This allows the free flow of creative manifestation energies. But vulnerability fears often cause us to fixate on imperfections, blocking alignment. Gratitude journaling shifts our gaze toward assets and abundance already present, rather than faults. It lifts us from a place of lack to one of overflowing fullness by choosing daily to think and feel grateful.

Gratitude also cultivates the emotional flexibility needed for successful manifestation. We all experience difficult times when focusing on the positive isn't instinctive. But training our minds through consistent journaling strengthens our gratitude muscles, so they function even during pain. This mental flexibility grants resilience to keep desires aligned with the source despite challenges. It opens us to trusting that life's ups and downs are perfectly unfolding.

Journaling gratitude develops vulnerability toward life by exercising faith that things will continually go our way if we stay loose and receptive rather than rigidly attached to outcomes. Vulnerability means allowing for life's twists and turns with an open hand. Gratitude journaling models this receptive approach, which sets the stage for co-creative manifestation energies to guide circumstances gently toward the highest good.

Expressing thanks also builds trust between ourselves and benevolent divine forces. Vulnerability depends on believing we'll receive help even when we're afraid, instead of barricading parts of ourselves away from help out of distrust. But journaling regularly shares gratitude for both small joys and greater miracles already manifested. Over time, this exercise deepens our trusting relationship with supportive powers, who always work on our behalf when we make space for them.

Gratitude additionally strengthens community connections, which are integral to manifestation. Sharing our journals' highlights with loved ones fosters closer bonds of mutual appreciation and care. It also encourages us to recognize support from people who are aiding life's beauty, which we've manifested so far. Communities hold us up, especially during tougher times, but vulnerability and open communication are needed to accept help graciously when offered.

Some guidance for starting a gratitude journal:

- Devote 5–10 minutes daily to write two to five specific things you're grateful for that day without overthinking.

- Variety makes journaling engaging long-term—appreciating nature, people, lessons learned that week, talents, health, and more.

- Include small daily pleasures alongside greater life gifts to maintain perspective during hardships.

- Review entries weekly to track blessings and shifts in perspective over time.

- Share selected entries periodically with supportive friends and family to spread gratitude.

Consistency enhances journaling's benefits. Stick with it through times when entries feel pointless—that's when practicing gratitude matters most for staying positive. Remember, maintaining perspective takes practice but yields rewards like better mental and emotional well-being and alignment for successful manifestation. Focusing on light within yourself and from others opens greater light in your way.

Gratitude Rituals for Vulnerability

While journaling is a powerful way to cultivate gratitude, ritual practices can deepen the experience even more. Rituals integrate energy, intention, and embodiment to nourish spiritual growth.

A Morning Ritual

Upon waking, sit quietly for five minutes, expressing heartfelt thanks for another day to live your truths courageously. You might say, "I appreciate this new morning with all its potential. Thank you for giving me insight and strength to walk bravely as my whole self today." Breathe deeply, feeling gratitude fill your body.

A Work Ritual

During lunch or breaks, step outside if the weather permits. Close your eyes and take three slow, deep breaths of fresh air while mentally thanking your lungs, heart, and entire system for their dedicated service despite vulnerabilities and stresses. You might say, "I am grateful to my heart, lungs, and overall system for their constant strength in the face of stress and vulnerability." Re-centered, return focused yet relaxed.

An Evening Ritual

Before sleep, make a gratitude tea or warm drink. As it steeps, think of one interaction where you showed vulnerability authentically, whether well received or not. With compassion, give thanks for lessons learned through the experience toward building stronger relationships and self-trust. Sip slowly, feeling gratitude nourish you inside and out.

A Weekly Ritual

On your chosen day of rest, prepare a gratitude snack or small meal. Selectively plate your favorite energizing foods, purposely including variety, representing diversity within yourself to fully appreciate. Throughout the meal, consciously embody feelings of appreciation for all parts that compromise your beautiful wholeness.

A Spontaneity Ritual

Whenever you experience vulnerability fears, pause to feel your quickened heartbeat or tense muscles. Take a few grounding breaths while mentally thanking your body for warning signals protecting perceived flaws. Release pressure at your own pace through breaths until relaxed again in patience with your process.

Rituals anchor deepening gratitude through tangible sensory experiences that nourish on levels beyond intellect. Taking time for ritual acknowledges life's passage marked by regular patterns punctuating timelessness. Make rituals sacred by giving your full presence without distraction to cultivate present-moment appreciation.

Further Tips

Keep rituals simple enough to repeat comfortably. Vary locations and times according to circumstance. Involve symbolic objects like candles, flowers, or photos if you wish. Note feelings and insights after rituals in a journal to track their impact on vulnerability over time. Welcome partner and community rituals when trusting connections form.

By integrating regular gratitude rituals attentively, vulnerability feels progressively more natural through practiced embodied wisdom. Rituals nourish courage's roots with lightness so it may bloom unrestrained. Combined with daily journaling, try incorporating several gratitude rituals tailored to your energy flow. Appreciation's practice transforms vulnerability from an abstract goal into a living breath, nourishing all life within and beyond.

Chapter 6:

Beyond Positive Thinking—The

Role of Emotions

Our feelings and emotions play a much bigger role in manifesting than we realize. Think about it: whenever you've manifested something amazing in your life, whether it was a new job, a special relationship, or healing from illness, there was likely an emotional experience that accompanied it. You probably felt excited, hopeful, grateful, or even relieved. These good feelings fueled the manifestation process. Likewise, when you've manifested something you didn't want, like an argument with a friend or your car breaking down, strong negative emotions like stress, anger, or sadness were probably part of the mix.

Our emotions aren't just reactions to our circumstances; they actually shape our reality. The vibration of our feelings sends powerful messages to the universe about what we think we deserve. When we feel worried, resentful, or unworthy on the inside, even if we're smiling and saying affirmations, that low emotional vibration matches up with experiences that validate those feelings. But when we open our hearts to emotions like joy, compassion, and appreciation, we tune ourselves to co-create events that nourish our soul.

The problem is that most of us weren't taught healthy ways to process our feelings growing up. Instead of being shown how to soothe our fears, release anger constructively, or embrace sadness, we were often told to put on a brave face or cheer up. Over time, this caused many of us to disconnect from our emotional truth and lose touch with what really makes us feel alive. And without awareness of what's stirring below the surface, we manifest from a place of reactivity instead of choice.

But it's never too late to get reacquainted with your feelings. It may sound tedious, but committing to checking in daily to see how you truly feel is so important for conscious manifestation. Start by sitting quietly and asking yourself, "What emotions am I experiencing right now, even if they're uncomfortable ones?" Then, follow each feeling with curiosity instead of judgment. Notice where you feel it in your body without trying to change it. This simple practice of emotional awareness will serve you so well on your manifestation journey.

Once you start tuning into your emotions, the next step is learning how to shift out of negative ones in a healthy, sustainable way. The most common thing people do when feeling bad is try to push it away with distractions or positive thinking, but this usually backfires in the long run. Unaddressed feelings have a way of bubbling back up when we least expect it, sabotaging our manifestations. A much more effective strategy is to feel your feelings fully through tools like journaling, talking to understanding friends, meditation, exercise, or creative expression like art, music, or dance.

Gently exploring the root causes of difficult emotions through reflection and surrounding yourself with uplifting people who accept you exactly as you are can also help immensely. When you make peace with the full spectrum of your humanity—the light and the dark— transformation happens naturally. The energy previously locked up in avoidance or positive thinking is unleashed to flow through you freely, attracting only situations and people that harmonize with your healed vibration.

It's also crucial to learn how to nurture good emotions like joy, optimism, compassion, and excitement. Smiling alone won't cut it; you need to intentionally fuel these uplifting feelings through activities you find genuinely fulfilling. Spending quiet time in nature, expressing gratitude, enjoying hobbies and acts of service, and connecting deeply with people who understand you can all work wonders. Make it a daily habit to nourish your emotional well-being, not just check off positive affirmations.

Manifestation is ultimately an inside job that happens through conscious energy management rather than surface thoughts or words alone. When you take the time each day to feel through what's really going on within you—both wonderful and painful—and set healthy boundaries, it will radically transform your ability to outwardly create what enriches your life. Your true desires flow from how you honestly feel at your joyful best. So, never fear or suppress your feelings, but instead embrace them as wise messengers guiding you home.

The Thoughts-Emotions Connection

We need to acknowledge that thoughts and emotions are not separate; they're two sides of the same coin. Our thoughts trigger emotions, and our emotions influence the stories we tell ourselves. It works like this: Every day, our minds are constantly generating thought after thought. Many of these thoughts are habitual worries, judgments, or negative self-talk that have been ingrained over the years. But we usually aren't fully aware of these underlying thought patterns.

The Cooperation Between Thoughts and Emotions

When certain thoughts arise, they trigger an emotional reaction based on how we've been conditioned to perceive events. For example, if a thought like "I'm not good enough" pops into your head, it will likely make you feel anxious, sad, or unworthy as a result. Your emotions then serve as feedback on the validity of that thought. The trouble is, most of us weren't taught as kids to question our thoughts. So, we often end up believing those initial distressing interpretations and reactions without realizing there could be another way to look at things.

From there, the negative thought-emotion cycle goes into effect. You feel bad, so you pay more attention to other thoughts that confirm why you're feeling bad. These emotions then fuel more stories, memories, and future projections, emphasizing lack, loss, or danger. Before long, you've completely bought into a limiting story about yourself or your circumstances without stopping to look at any counter-evidence. A sad or stressful feeling becomes the new normal emotional backdrop that tints how you experience life.

On the flip side, positive thoughts also trigger positive emotions, and vice versa. Suppose a kind friend pays you a nice compliment. The thought "I'm worthy of love" may arise, sparking feelings of confidence, joy, or gratitude. These good vibes then inspire more empowering stories about your abilities and potential. This optimistic emotion and thought feedback loop creates a frame of mind where you naturally notice opportunities and blessings wherever you turn.

The implications for manifestation are enormous. Whatever story we end up believing about ourselves on a feeling level shapes what kind of realities our energy can align with. If low self-worth or anxiety are predominant emotions, that thin emotional vibration will attract situations reflecting these states. But with practice, we can absolutely influence our thought patterns to shift into a higher emotional state more conducive to dreaming up our soul's desires.

Emotional Intelligence

This is where developing emotional intelligence comes in. Emotional intelligence refers to our ability to recognize and manage our own emotions, as well as understand and influence the emotions of others. It involves skills like self-awareness, self-regulation, empathy, motivation, and social skills. People with strong emotional intelligence are better equipped to interrupt limiting thought-emotion cycles and consciously redirect their feelings through mindful choices.

Self-Awareness

The first step in emotional intelligence is gaining self-awareness about your emotions. This means regularly checking in with how you truly feel beneath surface thoughts and behaviors, noticing physical sensations, and identifying what factors tend to trigger different reactions. Keeping an emotional diary can make unconscious beliefs and patterns more visible over time. Self-awareness also involves reflecting on your motivations—are you acting from a genuine place or to please others?

Self-Regulation

Once you see your inner landscape more clearly, self-regulation comes into play. This skill helps you manage disruptive emotions in the moment before they escalate your experience. Grounding techniques like deep breathing, visualizing safe spaces, or tapping acupressure points can create calm when big feelings arise, so you don't just react habitually. Journaling, talking to understanding friends, meditation, and exercise also aid in the release of stagnant emotions.

Empathy

Empathy is another pillar of emotional intelligence that supports manifestation. It involves considering other perspectives thoughtfully before judging, acknowledging feelings you may not agree with, and communicating caring support. Empathic people cultivate warm, trusting bonds by reading emotional cues and showing compassion. These strong social ties form a safety net that reduces stress, as well as a community to not only celebrate successes with but also assist in problem-solving life's curveballs.

Motivation Regulation

Motivation regulation means steering yourself toward constructive goals by channeling diffuse feelings like boredom into meaningful pursuits you care about. You can also use emotions strategically—for example, harnessing enthusiasm to brainstorm new opportunities or leveraging frustration productively into solutions instead of resistance. Influencing others' emotions ethically helps resolve conflicts and inspire participation through understanding different worldviews.

As you continue to develop self-awareness, self-control, empathy, and motivation skills, your ability to mindfully intervene in the thoughts-feelings cycle skyrockets. You gain autonomy over your emotional state instead of reacting on autopilot. When negative feelings do arise, you possess the competencies to thoughtfully determine their validity and reframe them productively if needed. This supports shifting into alignment with preferred realities tied to feeling purposeful, optimistic, and connected—the vibrations that manifest dreams.

Some helpful techniques for consciously practicing emotional intelligence are journaling prompts, meditation on emotional triggers, cognitive reframes, challenging beliefs, and compassionate self-talk. Visualization of ideal scenarios and gratitude for present blessings also lift vibrations. Surrounding yourself with growth-minded people, doing acts of service for others in need, and finding creative pastimes you find meaningful all nourish your emotional well-being further. With dedicated attention and self-care, raising your emotional IQ sets the stage for authentically conscious manifestation.

Understanding our thought and emotion dynamics sheds light on how we can exercise more choice over vibrational states attracting experiences. By developing key emotional intelligence competencies like awareness, regulation, empathy, and motivation over time, we gain the footing to question limiting thought patterns and redirect feelings in a healing way. This supports tuning into resonance with the vibrant realities of health, love, and purpose that nourish the soul. Your emotions have so much wisdom to offer when you make space to listen non-judgmentally.

Integrating Emotional Intelligence into Manifestation

We discussed how thoughts and feelings influence one another in a never-ending cycle, and emotional intelligence can help us consciously lead that cycle. Well, let's look at some tangible ways to strengthen specific emotional intelligence skills that fuel manifestation success.

Cultivating Self-Awareness

Self-awareness is the foundation of it all. Self-awareness involves noticing how you truly feel beneath surface behaviors and pinpointing what triggers certain reactions. Why is this important for creating what you want? Well, if we can't identify the emotions powering us at any given moment, we'll just keep attracting the same unpleasant surprises based on unconscious vibrations. But when you make feeling your emotions a daily meditation through reflection, old hurtful patterns loosen their grip.

A great self-awareness exercise is journaling prompts tailored for manifestation, like "What abundance feels like to me" or "How I can support myself during uncertainty." Freewriting answers let buried beliefs float to light for examination. Notice body sensations too—where do you hold tension, signaling buried feelings needing care? Self-awareness also means truly listening without judgment to how others perceive you and then weighing whether internal narratives match reality. With practice, you'll gain tremendous clarity on your emotional truth.

Developing Self-Regulating

This foundation of knowing yourself inside out allows for the next key skill: self-regulation. Being able to manage disruptive emotions before they hijack your experience is so important because reactions beyond your control block your highest manifestations. When big feelings arise, practice grounding techniques to create separation and calm, like deep breathing, tapping sore spots, visualizing safe havens, or replaying soothing memories.

Journaling is a powerful way to self-soothe through the release of expressing how you honestly feel without editing. Speaking to compassionate friends about what's weighing on your heart also dissipates energy stuck in avoidance. Regular meditation trains the mind to disengage from runaway thoughts fueling feelings and instead anchor presence in the present moment. Physical outlets like exercise, dance, and hiking in nature burn anxiety, so light and self-love can enter. With a commitment to these calming practices, you gain increasing control over your inner weather.

Cultivating Empathy

Another emotional intelligence hero for manifestation is empathy—the ability to consider different perspectives thoughtfully before judging, acknowledge how others may feel, even if it's uncomfortable, and offer caring support through active listening. When stressed, people often react harshly without thinking about how that affects those they care about most. But cultivating empathy ensures social ties remain sources of encouragement as you pursue goals, not extra burdens.

Make a point to regularly check in with loved ones in a way that invites vulnerability, such as asking, "How are you really doing?" instead of just small talk. Try replaying conversations from their perspective to gain insight into how your words land. Volunteer acts of service help you step outside your ego into others' shoes through compassion. Affirming cards, cooking a meal, or tending someone's garden when they need support creates feel-good bonds, powering manifestation.

Developing Motivation Regulation

Motivation regulation is also key—channeling amorphous emotions like boredom or restlessness into meaningful pursuits and goals that connect your talents to a better world. Inspire your manifestation through ethical actions that fuel purpose. Taking on volunteer roles, applying skills you enjoy, or mentoring someone lifts spirits even in tough times by shifting focus from outside worries onto meaningful contributions. Visualizing stepping bravely into your calling lights a fulfilling fire within, overcoming doubts through tiny steps and building momentum.

With committed practice raising these emotional intelligence muscles daily through various activities, you gain true autonomy over your experience. Negative thought spirals lose their grip as you become the warm, compassionate best friend to yourself through trusting inner guidance. Relationships deepen into cheerleader squads, carrying you through challenges with love. And motivation no longer wavers because you stay tethered to your inner knowing of your gifts' power to uplift humanity. From that unshakeable, centered place of emotional mastery arises unstoppable manifestation magic.

Recognizing and Processing Difficult Emotions

Recognizing feelings, especially uncomfortable ones, can be tricky. Plus, just feeling things isn't enough; we have to find healthy ways to actually work through them. So, let me share some insights on common inner blocks to the manifestation of success, like fear, doubt, and resistance. I'll also give you tools for identifying any emotional obstacles and gently dismantling them.

Fear

One of the biggest inner detractors many of us face is fear. It's totally normal to be afraid of putting ourselves out there, pursuing big changes, or facing the unknown as we manifest goals. But harboring unconscious fears like "I'm not good enough" or "I'll fail" holds us back through limited beliefs and keeps us playing it safe in mediocrity instead of exploring our true potential.

Here are some ways to shine a light on fearful emotions blocking your aspirations: Write a stream-of-consciousness piece about your deepest vulnerabilities. Speak aloud to supportive people so they lose power over you. Journal prompt answers help surface common fears around certain topics too ("What do I really fear about public speaking?"). Remember, fears thrive in darkness, so bringing them into awareness with kindness dissolves their grip.

From there, it's all about processing fear gently without repressing or distracting from it. Visualization works like magic here. Picture walking through feared situations with confidence and grace through small challenges you can actually take. Meditating on feelings of security, courage, and embrace helps override old fearful patterns. Writing compassionate letters to your inner, fearful child soothes wounds too.

Gradually facing fears through exposure grows you into someone at peace with uncertainty as you soar to new heights.

Doubt

Another common inner saboteur is doubt, which we don't mostly even realize. Questioning ourselves instead of celebrating our capacities attracts a lack of reality. Rooting out unconscious doubt takes reflection; notice automatic thoughts hindering you and where they stem from ("Did someone in my past make me feel incapable?"). Be willing to uncover old self-beliefs that no longer serve you. Journal prompts provide insights; for example, writing out the fears behind doubt illuminates core vulnerabilities for care.

Process doubt through self-validating affirmations and visualization of scenarios where you feel truly capable and supported. Ask trusted allies to point out evidenced times you succeeded too. Inner child letter writing or meditation on feelings of confidence undermines doubt over time. Notice automatic doubts arising and shift thoughts to more empowering self-talk with practice. Celebrating tiny steps instead of waiting for perfection builds unshakable belief in your light.

Resistance

Resistance is another tricky emotion we may not recognize as holding us back. It can disguise itself as rationalization, procrastination, or seeking distractions from opportunities. But resistance essentially happens when we ignore inner urgings for growth out of comfort with the status quo or fear of the unknown.

To identify resistance inside, be aware of tendencies to shrink from risk or continually put off what excites you for later. Notice energy changes in your body when considering expansion. Journaling facilitates recognizing rationalizations you make ("I'm too busy now"). Gently observing resistance allows you to compassionately ask what it's protecting and how to address its needs safely. Visualize stepping bravely into possibilities as resistance fades with the willingness to sit in the discomfort of the unknown a bit longer each time. Developing insight and patience with resistance instead of judgment helps relinquish control in faith.

These are some common inner players hampering manifestation. With tools like reflective journaling, visualization, talking to caring souls, and acts of self-care, you gain the ability to respectfully acknowledge fears, doubts, or resistance lurking inside. This awareness opens spaces to compassionately process emotions hindering your blossoming instead of letting them fester into habitual patterns of limitation.

Harnessing Positive Emotions

While no one emotion is inherently better than another, cultivating positive states aligns your energy with possibilities instead of problems. So, get ready to learn simple yet powerful exercises to encourage uplifting energies to flow through your experience:

- **One amazing way to access positivity is visualization.** Picture scenarios where you feel truly fulfilled and confident— being congratulated after a big win, spending quality time with loved ones, engaging in hobbies—bringing you into a flow state. Visually imagine details like surroundings, conversations, and physical sensations to make the vision real for your mind and body. Focus on appreciating the vision fully instead of just envisioning desired outcomes alone. This trains your subconscious to associate satisfaction with aspects of your preferred reality that are now in focus.

- **Another great visualization is depicting your ideal daily routine, where you feel happy, healthy, and productive while following your bliss.** Imagine accomplishing rewarding tasks with ease and enjoying leisure time, restoring your spirit. Imagine interactions with others going smoothly as you freely operate from an inner place of abundance, acceptance, and light. Dwelling in fantasies of thriving empowers your energy to attract circumstances, allowing visions' fulfillment in perfect timing.

- **Gratitude journaling raises vibrations fast by anchoring attention on life's blessings, often overlooked in worries.** Set aside 15 minutes each night before bed to record at least five things you felt grateful for that day, whether major or minor. Note how acknowledging even basic comforts and kindness lifts your mood with each entry. Gratitude compiles evidence against any feelings of lack, thereby disarming limitation and opening your channel to receive more. Consider expanding journals into gratitude vision boards or scrapbooks by pasting pictures representing gifts in your life.

- **Another incredibly effective method is affirming self-acceptance and capabilities daily.** Choose at least five short, heartfelt statements about inherent worth, gifts, or qualities you appreciate recognizing in yourself. Repeat them throughout the day, especially when doubt creeps in or after negative self-talk. Adding variations keeps affirmations fresh. Affirmations infuse the subconscious with empowering self-beliefs through focused repetition over time. Make affirmations uplifting yet believable to avoid disconnect; aim to validate inherent talents versus superficial traits alone.

- **Laughter releases feel-good neurotransmitters and lifts any stuck-low vibrations.** Keep a running joke book to brighten days and share lighthearted moments with others. Spend time with humorous friends who inspire giggles. Watch funny videos or comedies to trigger facial expressions, activating the humor response when loneliness creeps in. Laughter buffers stress and brings a fresh outlook on challenges through joyful mindset shifts. Even fake laughter boosts mood through the effort!

- **Another manifestation powerhouse is practicing gratitude toward others.** Small acts of expressing thanks to supportive souls nourish relationships, serving as safety nets through difficulties. Send short appreciation texts daily, reminding someone how much you value them. Drop off thoughtful gifts or homemade treats for busy people, uplifting you from afar too. Handwritten thank-you cards also build uplifting bonds, as does simply making time each week for quality conversations where people feel really heard.

Harnessing positive emotions requires a commitment to infusing daily activities with purposeful mindfulness. But consciously cultivating optimism, appreciation, acceptance, and joy reaps immense rewards by aligning your vibrant essence with all life desires gracing you amid blessings already here, waiting for notice. Don't hesitate to experiment until you find exercises sparking your light—that spark holds the power to manifest magic.

Emotional Release and Healing Practices

While acknowledging and managing feelings is important, it's also crucial to provide release valves for pent-up emotions stored in our bodies that affect energetic flow. That's why I want to introduce you to safe, natural practices to dissolve limiting energy patterns at their root.

Expressive Writing

Expressive writing is one of the simplest yet most impactful ways to release emotions through journaling prompts, freely expressing how you feel without editing yourself. Regularly devoting 15–30 minutes to stream-of-consciousness dumping about anything on your mind releases mental toxins that clutter thoughts and attract unwanted realities. Allow any feelings to come up without analysis, then observe how energy shifts after getting them out of your head and onto paper. Over time, this safe outlet dissipates worries, so calmer perspectives emerge naturally.

Yoga

Yoga also deeply sooths emotions through body-mind integration. Gentle stretches activate the parasympathetic nervous system, relaxing your physical form as mindfulness redirects chatter into present-centered awareness of breath and sensations. Yoga trains mental discipline through focused breathing, lowering stress levels that block clear intuition. Certain poses, like child's pose, cat-cow flows, and simple twists, also alleviate energetic and emotional blockages by stimulating healing circulation and lymph flow through tension areas. Commit to a regular light practice, letting tension melt away and opening your being to vibrant creation.

Eye Movement Desensitization and Reprocessing

Eye movement desensitization and reprocessing (EMDR) aids in releasing distressing memories that no longer serve you well through guided side-to-side eye movements. With an EMDR therapist's help, bring a charged situation to mind as you follow their finger or light with your eyes. This bilateral stimulation engages both brain hemispheres, soothing the amygdala's alarm response to past trauma memories. Over several sessions targeting layered memories, EMDR washes energetic residue from traumatic imprints, dismantling related cognitive patterns that limit belief in your inherent goodness and capabilities today.

Somatic Experience

Somatic experience further assists in releasing emotional wounds through the body. With a certified practitioner, explore where certain feelings manifest physically through sensations, postures, and tensions. Consciously direct breath into tight areas to help the nervous system discharge residual energy, making trauma responses no longer advantageous. Like with EMDR, this gentle approach recognizes the innate self-healing wisdom within to process distress instinctually instead of rationally. Allowing the body to naturally soothe and integrate distress through small, regulated releases reestablishes balance.

Art Therapy

Art therapy creatively channels raw emotions pouring out through varied mediums. Freeform doodling, scribbling, painting, or crafting with no planned goal simply fosters emotional catharsis in a soothing, nonverbal way. Using different colors, textures, shapes, and movements with different tools further engages both hemispheres of the brain for holistic release. Some find certain mediums especially cathartic, so experiment openly until intuitive, which aligns your expression for perspective shifts. Reviewing pieces later provides insights into patterns ready for conscious release.

Music Therapy

Music therapy also blends emotional processing beautifully into daily life. Simply playing, singing, or drumming freely to feelings releases tension physically while guiding the breath into a meditative flow state. Listening selectively with awareness of how certain genres affect your state allows conscious selection, aiding release or lifting low moods into empowerment. Create playlists tailored for processing intense feelings, upbeat motivation, or soothing worries. Instruments provide catharsis through freeform playing that is non-musically aligned to the inner rhythm. Over time, daily musical connection grounds peace and surrender.

While not a complete treatment for clinical issues alone, expressive, artistic, and body-focused release practices promote natural healing from painful holdings when consistently incorporated. With patience and care for yourself, devotedly applying these techniques regularly reprograms thought and physical responses to past difficulties, liberating flow for the present. Your inherent resilience shines through to align all areas with well-being, manifesting beauty from within outwardly as flowers follow the sun.

Chapter 7:

The Art of Letting Go—Releasing

Resistance

Resistance is anything that works against our goals and desires. It can be negative thoughts, limiting beliefs, attachments to certain outcomes, or a fear of lack or loss. As long as we resist what we want to manifest, the universe cannot bring it to us easily. It's like trying to push two magnets together when their same poles are facing—there will be friction. In the same way, when we resist what we want with our thoughts and energy, it creates friction that stops the manifestation process.

So, how do we release this resistance? The key is learning to let go, to surrender to the process, and to trust that we will receive what is best for us in the best possible way. Letting go is crucial for manifestation because it allows the natural flow of energy to bring us what we truly want without our ego or fear getting in the way. When we let go of resistance, we allow the manifestation to happen easily and effortlessly.

I know letting go may sound difficult. After all, we are so used to controlling our lives and outcomes. But surrendering does not mean giving up or being passive. It simply means accepting what is, having faith, and allowing the magic to unfold in its own unique way and perfect timing. When we surrender, we shift our energy from one of frustration or force to one of calm, openness, and receptivity. We make space for what we want to come through.

Think of it as flowing water in a river; it can either flow smoothly downstream or meet resistance in the form of rocks and bends. When we fight the current or try to control it with force, it creates turbulence. But when we surrender to the natural flow and direction, the water moves with ease. In the same way, when we try to force or control our manifestations with worry or impatience, we create inner turbulence that hinders the process. But when we surrender control and have faith in a higher plan, things start flowing effortlessly toward us.

Some common ways our minds resist what we want to manifest include impatience, doubt, worry, fear of lacking or losing something, attachment to specific outcomes, overthinking scenarios, and the need for control. These thoughts create resistance frequencies that repel our desires. Some people are even resistant without realizing it; deep down, they may feel unworthy of having good things happen, or that success or happiness can lead to negative consequences. This unconscious resistance is the hardest to identify, but letting go is key to dissolving it.

The challenge is that once we identify resistance within, it takes practice to let go of those patterns. We have to catch ourselves replaying negative or controlling tapes in our minds and consciously swap them for relaxed, open thoughts. Anytime we feel the tension coming up, we can soothe it with deeper breathing and affirmations. With regular practice, letting go gets easier, and your manifestations will start flowing in quickly.

Some techniques for releasing resistance include meditation, journaling, dancing, spending time in nature, sharing with a friend, saying daily affirmations, envisioning the end result, or taking inspired action toward your goals. These activities shift you to a higher frequency where resistance cannot exist. Regular practice helps you get comfortable with the uncertain nature of manifestation and releases attachment to specific outcomes.

You also need to let go of comparing your journey to others. Two people asking for the same thing may receive it in very different ways and timings. Surrender to trusting that what's meant for you will come through in a way that serves your highest good. Letting go of judgment empties your cup so the universe can continuously fill it.

It is not easy to simply flip a switch and fully release resistance. Be gentle and compassionate with yourself as you work through lingering doubts. Remember, you have the power within to dissolve resistance with awareness and consistency. Loving yourself through the ups and downs will serve you far better than self-criticism ever could. This journey is about having faith in a benevolent universe and an infinite well of creativity within you. Stay determined yet relaxed as you practice letting it all unfold.

Know that you already have everything you need within you to manifest your desires. And also, the world and the universe have everything you need to manifest your desire. The more you can release resistance by surrendering control and trusting in a higher plan, the easier it will become to actualize your dreams. Letting go is key to overcoming inner and outer obstacles effortlessly. Be patient yet consistent; with time, you will amaze yourself with the ease and speed at which your manifestations appear.

Understanding Resistance in Manifestation

To truly grasp how manifestation works, we must shine a light on the concept of resistance. Resistance plays a key role as a barrier that stops our desires from coming to pass with ease. It creates friction in a process that is meant to flow smoothly.

In simple terms, resistance refers to any thought, belief, or feeling within us that defies what we want to bring into reality. It acts as an energetic blockade that repels our goals and dreams, keeping them at a distance rather than allowing them to be drawn near. Resistance comes in many subtle forms, both conscious and unconscious. Most of the time, we may not even notice we are resisting until certain patterns emerge.

Some common types of resistance include doubt, fear, worry, impatience, attachment to specific outcomes, lack mentality, comparison to others, overthinking, control issues, and feelings of unworthiness.

- Doubt in our ability to manifest creeps in when we fear something may not work out.

- Fear arises from the unknown or concern about change.

- Worry takes us into anxious scenarios about what could go wrong.

- Impatience stems from wanting results immediately without appreciation for the process.

- Attachment to a single desired outcome rather than its essence resists flexibility.

- Lack mentality, comparison, and unworthiness whisper that we are not deserving or doomed for failure.

- Overthinking analyzes timelines, details, and exceptions rather than trusting the natural flow.

- Control issues wrest power from the universe by demanding rigid outcomes our way.

These inward strains generate resistant frequencies that magnetically repel the object of our manifestation in both subtle and obvious ways.

On an energetic level, resistance creates inner turmoil that disrupts the smooth flow of life force needed to manifest our hearts' dreams. It generates static interference akin to holding two magnets facing the same charge; inner friction builds, preventing effortless union with our goals. When we externally blame outer factors or inwardly berate a lack of effort, resentment simmers within, further muddying energetic clarity. This turmoil within broadcasts a signal that repels our desires, keeping them distant like two opposing poles of a magnet.

Similarly, consciously or unconsciously uttering negative patterns aloud to friends, family, or even strangers continues to amplify the low vibrational frequencies we seek to transform. The law of assumption states that whatever we assume and hold true within ourselves will work to draw or repel experiences accordingly. By identifying resistance as a hindrance to our highest good and consciously shifting to faith and patience despite all, we clear inner mental space for new creations to be birthed.

Resistance also delays manifestation by prolonging the necessary inner work. It masks core issues we must recognize and heal to rise above lack-based consciousness once and for all. By resisting change, we resist growth and remain tethered to familiar but disempowering narratives despite our earnest visualization work. We instead dig deeper without realizing how this hinders outside circumstances from perfectly reflecting our highest awakened state. Realizing resistance permits transformation and accelerated manifestations by consciously dissolving its grip each day.

Struggle persists when we try forcefully pushing against the current rather than surrendering to the natural ebb and flow. By relaxing into the present flow and practicing daily release of attachment through journals, dancing, sharing, or similar techniques, we dissolve resistance accumulated over multiple lifetimes and timelines and realign for accelerated manifestation. With focused commitment, these invisible energetic weights that held us hostage for so long lose power as new, empowering patterns anchor in their place.

Understanding resistance revolutionizes our relationship with manifestation. No longer at its mercy, we command circumstances instead through conscious vigilance over our assumptions. With awareness, struggle surrenders to inspired action, impatience cedes to appreciation, and delay evolves into delight as we witness accelerated returns on minimal effort. Resistance demystified permits higher consciousness to be expressed rather than repressed through outer happenings. We emerge as enlightened co-creators fulfilling preordained potential across dimensions through continued practice, dissolving inner fears to externalize dreams.

The Art of Letting Go

Manifestation requires more than just visualizing our dreams; we must learn to release all attachments to outcomes and trust the natural flow. This is called "letting go," and it plays a pivotal role in removing resistance that hinders our desires from materializing. By surrendering control and beliefs of lack, we get out of the universe's way, so it can bring us our heart's deepest fulfillment. While sounding simple, learning to let go takes regular inner work and practice shifting out of habituated control modes. However, the rewards of releasing attachment truly accelerate manifestation through relaxed receptivity.

Benefits of Releasing Attachment

Some benefits of letting go include dissolving struggle as we cease wrestling with the current and instead flow harmoniously with natural rhythms. Rather than fearing lack, we tap into faith that infinitely creative forces guide circumstances perfectly. Trust replaces worry, so each twist surprisingly contributes to a grander, unseen plan. Surrender calms an anxious mind into present-moment peace instead of distressing over what-ifs. Flexibility replaces rigidity; we are more open to surprises than static outcomes.

Appreciation grows for small blessings as lack disappears behind gratitude's veil. We recognize life's beauty through simplicity rather than fixation on one path. Resentment surrenders to forgiveness as others' actions no longer dictate our serenity. Personal power emerges from relinquishing previous disempowering beliefs as something greater than ego uplifts us. Ultimately, letting go permits life magic to work effortlessly through us rather than us fruitlessly working against subtle energies.

Strategies for Letting Go

A key strategy is mindfulness: Briefly checking in periodically to observe any tension creeping back into thoughts and shifting focus from mental chatter or future worries to present sensations. Deep breathing soothes stress as we inhale calm and exhale unrest. We learn that brief discomfort passes while fulfilling our destiny remains, motivating relaxed determination. Gratitude lists counter lack mentality by appreciating what is rather than fixating on what is not yet.

Gentle movements like yoga or dancing release resistance held physically within the body. Nature exposure boosts ecological mindfulness of life's interconnectivity and our small role within it, inspiring humility and replacing pride's illusions. Expressive journaling sheds light on fears weighing mental energy down through non-judgmental awareness of underlying emotions. Conversations with supportive listeners release self-doubt as wise words reframe narratives.

The emotional freedom technique (EFT) offers an impactful strategy. It pairs tapping acupressure points with verbalizing an issue to clear its emotional charge. For example, "Even though I feel resistant to letting go of attachment to specific outcomes, I deeply love and accept myself." Tapping each endpoint, like the eyebrow or undereye, while repeating the issue dissolves its power through mind-body reconditioning. Combined with breathing, it melts away inner conflicts swiftly for peaceful clarity.

Imagery assists in shedding attachment by envisioning circumstances fulfilling goals in surprising yet benevolent ways beyond current expectations. This shifts the fixed assumptions holding us back. For example, visualizing feeling gratitude for something that recently appeared to go wrong but understanding its hidden blessing nurtures flexibility and openness to life's magic. Such practices dissolve resistance by releasing the perceived need for control into blissful cooperation with higher forces.

Core to any release work lies compassion—for ourselves in our humanness yet determination, and others acting from conditioned patterns unaware. Non-judgment nurtures forgiveness for lingering faults perceived and relieves unnecessary weight in the present. With compassion, mistakes become lessons, building wisdom rather than shame and corroding self-worth. We remember we are works-in-progress, as is all life—perfectionism exists not in outcome but in imperfect progress.

Most importantly, remember that letting go is a practice; we may slip, but gently return focus to blessings, breath, and recommit to faith that all is well and unfolding as it should. Compared to problematic behaviors, not letting go harms no one; use perceived failures compassionately to deepen understanding of resistance's subtleties and strengthen the resolve to live freely. Trust the process, be well, and let manifestation flow! May these insights support releasing fear through the loving sacrifice of ego's perceived control for your highest spiritual and material good.

Trusting the Process

Trust plays an important part in manifestation, yet it can be difficult to fully develop, especially when things don't seem to be moving as quickly as we hoped. However, maintaining faith in unseen forces guiding circumstances beautifully comprises an art worth refining for accelerated results. Deep down, we intuit that life obeys transcendent principles, yet anxiety chips at faith if light delays. Learning to wholly trust manifestation's mysterious ways replaces fears with gratitude for each step's purpose, however small, in fulfilling greater plans.

Benefits

Some benefits of trusting include experiencing less stress. Rather than obsessing over timelines or potential obstacles, relax, knowing everything contributes to the highest good. Tranquility cultivates the inner conditions for desires to manifest most easily. Trust permits acceptance of what is rather than frustration over delays, thus preserving positive energy and attracting goals. It nurtures patience during development phases, enhancing outcomes qualitatively rather than rushing unfinished products and missing vital lessons.

Trust lets go of micromanaging details beyond control. We cooperate with the flow instead of mentally grasping at straws in the dark. Faith recognizes all contributing causes align perfectly despite surface chaos, thus instilling meaning even through difficulties. It prevents resenting growth periods as unavoidable steps in a holistic journey. By embracing uncertainties, confident destinies unfold as intended, and life surprises joyously rather than disappointing rigid expectations.

Cultivating Trust

Developing trust takes practice—aligning thoughts with bigger truths. Start by identifying small everyday blessings often overlooked due to fixation on major wants. Pausing daily to consciously appreciate simple gifts cultivates gratitude, overshadowing doubt. Faith also strengthens, reflecting how previous prayers were answered, though originally disguised. This reveals patterns transcending three dimensions, proving life supports rather than sabotages its highest purposes.

Surrounding with trust reinforced subconsciously boosts when consciously felt. Spending time in nature reminds us of our smallness within a grand scheme, yet interdependence inspires humility, replacing arrogance and control fantasies. Associating with upbeat optimists lightens heavy burdens, reminding us that challenges too shall pass. In contrast, limiting exposure preserves faith threatened by constant gloomy prognostications. Reading inspirational materials reinforces wisdom guiding present mysteries seemingly senseless.

Creative visualization cultivates trust by imagining goals fulfilled in uplifting yet unpredicted ways. This shifts energy from problem-focused to solution-focused, attracting new pathways. Journaling boosts faith by revisiting past prayers answered, though disguised at the time. Noticing divine fingerprints hidden within seeming insignificance retroactively instills present direction. Speaking affirmative statements maintains an upbeat attitude, overriding doubts as natural as criticisms surfacing. Reciting mantras, prayers, or uplifting verses also soothes anxious wondering.

Affirming trust feels challenging yet profoundly rewarding when practiced consistently with patience. Reminding ourselves that worries stem from conditioning, not eternal truths, transforms anxious energy into inspired action aligned with the soul's purpose and excitement. Each reframes another rung, climbing faith's ladder, gaining a wider perspective, and unveiling life's invisible hand. With mindfulness redirecting habitual fright into fascinated anticipation, fresh solutions bloom.

Doubts arise due to impatience yet persist due to a lack of signs; tackle both by refocusing inwardly until outward proof manifests. Do today what energizes rather than what seems tangibly progressive, trusting that hidden rewards outweigh apparent costs. Combat uncertainties by nurturing intuition aligned with cosmic intelligence beyond thinking's limits. Note wise hunches pulling in satisfying directions as a distinction from fears masquerading. Feed budding sprouts of faith with daily water and sunlight to maintain focus, letting nature transform tiny seeds exponentially.

Trust takes baby steps, yet strides follow as the mind notices patterns confirming bigger plans at play. Though mysteries remain, believing light triumphs darkness dispels anxiety for solutions birthed from positive mind soil. Each practice aligns the subconscious with higher purposes, making way for dreams' fruition. With patience comes proof, transforming vision into tangible sight. May these tools bolster faith during life's unfolding adventures of growth guided by trust beyond sight and logic!

Embracing Uncertainty

Uncertainty is an inevitable part of human existence. However, most of us tend to see uncertainty as something problematic that we need to avoid or reduce. We want predictable routines and seek guarantees in life whenever possible. This desire for control and certainty is just an illusion, though. When we accept uncertainty as a natural part of life, it becomes much easier to handle whatever comes our way.

The Illusion of Control

Deep down, we all have this feeling that we can control outcomes if we plan carefully enough. This makes uncertainty seem threatening because it suggests things can happen that are outside of our control. While planning is useful, we underestimate how much is truly beyond our power to determine. So many factors influence our lives that we cannot account for, from chance events to other people's decisions. No matter how hard we try, complete control is impossible.

Rather than an illusion, accepting our lack of control can be freeing. It means not blaming ourselves if unexpected difficulties arise and not constantly worrying about unknown future problems. Life becomes less stressful when we stop believing we must secure every detail. Some uncertainty is reassuring too; it leaves room for pleasant surprises! Attempting to remove all uncertainty sets us up for frustration since this will never fully happen. A better approach is to make peace with unpredictability.

The Role of Uncertainty in Manifestation

Many people intuitively grasp that manifestation depends on embracing uncertainty. Manifestation requires envisioning a desired outcome but leaving space for an unspecified how it occurs. If we claim to know exactly how things must happen, it limits possibilities. An open mindset toward uncertainty expands creative potential. When we detach from rigid plans and expectations, we allow life's natural flow to bring circumstances together in auspicious ways.

Manifestation also relies on having an unwavering faith that things will work out, even without every step being clear. This faith requires being at peace with uncertainty—trusting that what needs to unfold will unfold in ways serving our highest good, even if unseen by us currently. With such an attitude, we welcome whatever opportunities or solutions come rather than fearing undesirable unknowns. Uncertainty paradoxically helps give power to our manifestation by relaxing control and inviting greater wholeness to emerge spontaneously in its own timing.

Reframing Perspectives on Uncertainty

Most people regard uncertainty negatively as something messy, problematic, or frightening. However, reframing how we view uncertainty can transform our relationship with it completely. A few simple shifts in perspective can help us embrace, rather than resist, the unknowns in life.

See uncertainty as natural, not abnormal. Recognizing unpredictability as a normal human experience relieves us of the notion that something is wrong when it arises. We accept that uncertainty belongs in life just as surely as certainty does.

Consider uncertainty an opportunity, not a threat. When we are open to possibilities rather than fearing a lack of answers, uncertainty excites our imagination rather than stressing it. We become curious about potential versus dreading undefined outcomes.

Trust that life will provide, even without having all the details mapped out. Faith in a benevolent universe nurtures confidence that whatever is meant to be will come our way without us having to orchestrate every step cognitively.

Focus on the present moment rather than worrying excessively about the future. We often cause needless suffering by dwelling on unknowns that may never happen. By appreciating what is happening now, uncertainty loses power over our peace.

Gain perspective by seeing uncertainty as growth-inducing rather than frustrating. Struggles with ambiguity strengthen flexibility, resilience, and creativity over-reliance only on structured processes. They help us develop as whole, multifaceted individuals.

See uncertainty as a chance to deepen compassion and empathy for others in similar situations rather than feeling anxious. Knowing life's road has mysterious twists for everyone cultivates patience and kindness.

With a shift in the inner lens, uncertainty transforms from adversary to friend and even benefactor. A welcoming approach reduces feelings of being victims to unpredictability, restoring our power to meet uncertainty and thrive within its territory. Embracing uncertainty with reassuring perspectives is what helps us manifest our highest visions for living optimally, joyously, and without undue fear or constraint.

Aligning with the Flow

Each of us experiences moments when everything seems to move effortlessly without stress or struggle. Tasks are accomplished with ease, and time vanishes as we are fully absorbed. This state of optimal experience is known as "flow." Understanding flow provides insight into how to navigate life in a smoother, more mindful manner aligned with natural energies. Flow is also fun, and having fun means being in the moment, which means having flow.

Defining Flow and its Significance

The concept of flow was described by psychologist Mihaly Csikszentmihalyi, who found it occurs when individuals are fully immersed in an activity requiring their focused skills (Cherry, 2023). In flow, people are challenged just at the outer edge of their abilities, where stretching happens without being overwhelmed. They have clear goals and receive immediate feedback about their efforts. Self-consciousness fades, and the sense of time is distorted until the present moment, which is all that seems to exist in a harmonious trance-like state.

Flow is like being carried on a current of energy rather than forcing our way upstream against resistance. When we operate in sync with the inherent streams of life rather than attempting to control them rigidly, we enter a relaxed yet highly productive rhythm. Flow has benefits for the body, mind, and soul. It reduces stress and lifts moods as the mind is too engaged to dwell on problems. Long-term flow allows the cultivation of mastery through absorption in meaningful pursuits we're passionate about. This holistic engagement of skills and challenges at the moment holds meaning greater than itself.

The Relationship Between Flow and Manifestation

The principles of flow resonate deeply with manifestation. To manifest is to align our intentions with universal creative currents, so that what we envision naturally flows into form. Several facets of flow enhance manifestation abilities:

- **Clear goals and immediate feedback:** To enter flow, it requires setting focused but open-minded objectives, and then responding to situational cues. This mirrors manifesting with specific yet adaptable aims and sensitivity to signs instead of rigid rigidity.

- **Challenges at skill level:** Flow happens at the edge of competence where talents are stretched, mirroring manifestation's reliance on courage to aspire beyond current limits and catalysts for growth.

- **Absorption in the process:** In flow and effective manifestation, we lose fixation on endpoints and place prime importance on enjoying the present unfolding, allowing higher wisdom to oversee results.

- **Surrender of self-consciousness:** Flow demands letting go of inhibitions around the judgment of ourselves or others, fostering compassion essential for manifesting for the collective highest good rather than personal shallow ego gratification alone.

- **Experiencing timelessness:** Flow alters perceptions of scheduling, just as manifestation knows divine timing beyond human schedules will actualize goals as conditions ripen at their own pace.

By cultivating flow in daily living and creative activities, we embrace manifestation's requisites of clear purpose combined with adaptability, trust beyond superficial plans, and relaxation into life's carrier rhythm. The following flow facilitates manifestation as surely as tides follow the lunar push-and-pull.

Integrating Flow into Daily Life

Given flow's benefits, it makes sense to consciously integrate elements supporting its emergence into the daily routine. The most important point about flow is having fun in life. A few suggestions for how this can be done while respecting the limits of energy or circumstances:

- Find activities engaging your skills and interests that can become flow-inducing habits, like exercise, artistic hobbies, playing with children, and spending time in nature.

- Schedule meaningful work that stretches your capacity but is not overwhelming in ways that allow full concentration. Take breaks to recharge when other responsibilities call.

- Pursue absorptive challenges by experience-seeking yet balancing enough risk to feel accomplished undertaking them, like learning new skills through classes or projects.

- Maintain gratitude journals, focusing on presence rather than resenting the past or anticipating the future. Practice mindfulness meditation to lower stress responses and raise flow potential wherever you are.

- Limit multi-tasking and technology distractions while engaged in priority core activities needing deep attention, such as studying, creating, or socializing face-to-face.

- Adjust yourself and your outer expectations realistically to your actual situation with compassion versus rigid goals that cause failure, anxiety, and defeating flow.

- Celebrate flow states by noting your experiences with them to cultivate appreciation and awareness, raising the likelihood of future occurrences.

- Cultivate receptivity to embrace life's unforeseen turns as valued growth instead of problems, allowing flow-friendly surrender of tightly held plans and narrow perspectives.

While always respecting practical responsibilities, small adjustments in daily rhythm, goals, and self-awareness can raise the odds of accessing flow spontaneously. By learning to cooperate rather than struggle against life's natural wisdom, we optimize the manifestation of the highest outcomes with less wasted effort.

Chapter 8:

Integration and Application

While gaining awareness of discrete concepts, it is equally important to integrate different pieces into a cohesive whole. A multifaceted understanding allows the most effective application to adapt to the diverse realities we all experience.

Manifesting requires not just intellectually grasping ideas but embodying wisdom in relationships, work, self-care, thoughts, and community involvement. Integration is key to confidently navigating unexpected situations that test flexibility without compromising principles. An integrated understanding also cultivates patience, as changes often happen gradually through our co-creative involvement.

Life presents us with a multitude of situations that call on diverse skill sets and states of awareness simultaneously. To genuinely thrive in complexity, we must develop an integrated consciousness drawing on life's different domains for balanced perspective and mutually supportive growth. Some benefits of such an outlook include

- seeing connections instead of separation between spheres usually categorized apart like career versus spirituality or self- versus others; this fosters synergy.

- appreciating the counterbalancing role various areas play in sustaining well-being, like the importance of downtime following periods of high productivity.

- accessing interdisciplinary wisdom for solving issues requiring consideration from multiple lenses, as no single solution alone can suffice.

- developing a non-compartmentalized sense of self not defined by any role alone but comprised of rich nuances fully embraced.

- feeling greater purpose guiding efforts across life terrain and deeper belonging to the human family when disparate spheres align with a shared conscience.

- weathering unexpected stressors from any area by flexibly drawing fortitude from other stable dimensions accordingly.

- acting with empathy and appreciation; diverse constraints shape unique paths and perspectives worthy of respect.

Manifestation exemplifies how an integrated perception enhances the capacity to actualize visions for positive change. Let's explore dimensions warranting mindful attention:

- **Physical health:** A balanced body supports well-being, and focus is essential for manifestation. Simple measures like nutritious eating, exercise, and rest help us inhabit energies creatively when life feels overwhelming.

- **Mental clarity:** An aware mindfulness countering negative assumptions or multitasking clutter facilitates manifestation's intuitiveness. Practices like meditation and journaling cultivate clear heads.

- **Emotional maturity:** Emotional intelligence, developed through vulnerability and community bonds, enables coping flexibility vital for manifestation amid external unpredictability.

- **Spiritual fulfillment:** A purpose- and values-driven life invites the empowerment of alignment with divine rhythm, manifesting life's meaning. Daily spiritual disciplines aid integration.

- **Social contribution:** Giving back through compassion cultivates reciprocity by supporting communities and providing resources for manifestation journeys.

- **Financial sustainability:** Manifestors require basic security, meeting responsibilities, not depleting focus, or receiving society's welfare without giving value back purposefully.

- **Vocational engagement:** Work involving passions and utilizing talents nurtures productivity channels and skills for manifested ventures, yet is balanced with the above dimensions.

- **Environmental stewardship:** Manifestation considers the impact on the natural world, sustaining all life, which conditions also influence outer conditions and spirits. Conservationism helps integration.

- **Family commitment:** Manifestation promotes intergenerational wellness through nurturing relationships with dependents or ancestors upon whose shoulders one stands.

We are multidimensional beings deserving care across domains as an integrated whole greater than parts. An imbalance in priorities reduces efficiency across the spectrum. Manifestation then emerges organically from practiced awareness across the life arena in mutually fortifying ways.

The Holistic Badass Mindfulness Framework

The principles underlying badass mindfulness mesh together into an integrative framework guiding everyday living. At its core, the framework supports cultivating a holistic awareness across all dimensions of our being to actualize life dreams in alignment with universal energies.

Thought Awareness and Reframing

Our thoughts strongly influence reality since they shape interpretation, filtering life events and possibilities we consider. Awareness of mental habits empowers shifting limiting ideas, blocking manifestation. Some helpful approaches include:

- noting thought patterns automatically arising in different situations through reflection and journaling.

- catching negative or worrying thoughts that fuel anxiety instead of solutions and replacing them with hopeful and supportive alternatives.

- questioning thought distortions like "always" or "never" statements, which exaggerate outcomes without accounting for complexity.

- affirming strengths to the inner critic and embracing the diversity of perspectives, including in others.

- visualizing goals from the assumption of already having manifested them to embed possibility within the subconscious.

- reframing challenges into learning lessons or evidence of resilience, cultivating patience for divine timing instead of frustration.

With mindfulness, we reveal empowering beliefs contrary to limiting stories holding us back from embracing life's opportunities. Reframing provides space for discovering situations from more resourceful angles, aiding manifestation.

Emotional Intelligence and Regulation

Emotions hold valuable guidance if the meaning behind reactions is understood and accepted without judgment. However, excessive emotional indulgence or suppression curbs manifestation by clouding judgment or stifling self-expression's energy. Cultivating emotional skills involves:

- identifying a wide spectrum of feelings instead of relying on limited labels and their messages.

- experiencing emotions fully without getting swept in tidal waves deterring solutions but also not bottling them up.

- developing empathy to understand different emotional needs and responses in ourselves and others.

- using relaxation practices like belly breathing to manage emotional triggers more constructively in challenging situations instead of compulsive reactions.

Communicating feelings assertively without attacking enables honest assessment, supporting healthy bonding and cooperation that aligns interests. With regulation, we channel rich emotional guidance, constructively informing choices aligned with dignity and vision. This adds compassion to the daily navigation of life currents.

Intentional Action and Alignment

While awareness cultivates possibilities, tangible steps lining up actions with purpose render manifestation concrete. Living with intent involves:

- committing to small, consistent actions instead of grandiosity alone, so momentum compounds, achieving bigger things step-by-step.

- ensuring core daily activities serve priorities and passions identified as personally meaningful over unconscious drifting.

- willingness to leave limiting comfort zones and try diverse avenues inspired as potential growth catalysts.

- modifying planned actions adapting gracefully to life cues instead of rigidly sticking to strategies no longer applicable.

- connecting with a community of like-minded souls for mutual learning, accountability, and broader possibilities.

- practicing gratitude daily for blessings already received as a motivator and reminder of abundance, supporting further alignment.

Through intentional yet adaptable living, we pursue dreams wholeheartedly while also responsively flowing with unfolding changes manifesting each moment. This cultivates resilience in navigating surprises.

Vulnerability, Gratitude, and Trust

Core social skills enhance manifestation by inviting opportunities and support, including:

- Vulnerability through honest, non-defensive sharing of challenges and wins with trustworthy circles expands perspectives and multiplies empowerment.

- Daily gratitude for simple pleasures and others enriching lives cultivates positive perspectives, attracting more fulfillment.

- Compassion embraces diverse journeys, respecting humanity's shared struggle instead of competition or harsh judgment.

- Developing interdependence seeing the community as a family providing a care network in times of need as much as in times of plenty.

- Trusting in a benevolent life force greater than concrete problems or personal ego desiring and believing help exists where envisioned.

These relationship qualities help us see past apparent obstacles and realize dreams through cooperation aligned with life's cooperative spirit. They nourish intention with encouragement for continued growth.

By cultivating holistic awareness, our very consciousness expands, becoming a manifestation partner responsive to opportunities. This framework empowers honoring Earth's nourishing cycles and sustaining all beings. May we walk gently, work harmoniously and gratefully, and see each moment full of creative potential in service of life's beauty. When integration is our shared intention, then care, justice, and abundance will surely flourish for all.

Techniques for Badass Mindfulness

Manifestation involves consciously shaping our reality, which requires focused intent and specific tools. While mindful living principles lay the foundation, applying various techniques strengthens manifestation abilities.

Journaling

Writing provides an outlet for reflecting inward or outward. A manifestation journal details goals, thoughts, feelings, experiences, gratitude, and lessons learned. It encourages accountably tracking progress and realizing visions. Journaling also permits noticing how circumstances unfold over time, showing gradual changes occurring. The act of writing clarifies objectives and affirms intentions, while re-reading entries boosts motivation. Keeping a daily journal allows for a deeper manifestation mindset.

Affirmations

Affirmations are positive statements said confidently in the present tense as if desires have already happened, such as "I am now healthy and happy." Repeating affirmations causes the subconscious to accept goals naturally. They can be written or spoken while gazing at goal pictures for full mind-body experiences of attainment. Affirmations instill inspiration, overriding doubts. They are best personalized and concise for maximum impact. Saying them gratefully in mirrors, preferably in the mornings and evenings, locks in transformed self-perceptions. Tell yourself about these affirmations in a way that makes you believe them.

Visualization

Vividly envisioning objectives as accomplished and how surrounding circumstances will allow nourishing them mentally before physical manifestations. Visualization stimulates corresponding brain patterns, reinforcing new neural pathways. It cultivates faith that what is intended will come to pass since the mind cannot easily differentiate visualization from reality. Techniques like visual boarding or drawing out desires make them more concrete, while relaxation induced through deep breathing enhances visualization's focus and impact.

Breathing Exercises

Conscious breathing shifts the mind and body from stress to calm, which is indispensable for clear manifestation intent. Diaphragm breaths trigger the parasympathetic rest-and-digest response, counteracting tension accumulated from worries. Techniques like breath focus get oxygen into the bloodstream, nourishing every cell. They center our present awareness, minimizing disruptive past or future thoughts. Slowing the breath links mind and body states, reinforcing peaceful manifestation beliefs. Controlled exhalation, releasing stagnant energies, further prepares the system for receptivity.

Reframing

Negative thought patterns produce similar outer realities if left unchecked. Reframing cognitive distortions challenges such disempowering mindsets. It means perceiving circumstances from a growth-oriented perspective instead of constantly judging or blaming oneself or others. Events considered setbacks become learning lessons. Reframing turns problems into opportunities by optimistically brainstorming innovative solutions and moving goals forward. Affirming personal values and separating from situations helps as well, as does replacing "always" or "never" thoughts with a positive attitude.

Cognitive Restructuring

While reframing perceptions within problems, cognitive restructuring completely reworks unhelpful thought frameworks inhibiting well-being. For instance, replacing core beliefs of personal worthlessness with knowing one's inherent worth despite imperfections. It means exchanging mentalities of scarcity for abundance despite the current lack. Catastrophizing turns into cautious optimism. Cognitive restructuring establishes new mindsets that serve goals where prior attitudes remained limited. Doing the mental housework to identify illogical thoughts replaces them with evidence-aligned perspectives and a better-fulfilled personal vision.

Mindfulness Meditation

Meditation trains the ability to observe mental, emotional, and physical experiences non-reactively from a centered, spacious awareness. It fosters present-moment concentration, cutting past and future distractions, while exposure to persistent thoughts softens identification with their stories. As a result, meditators gain independence from thoughts pulling them off course. They respond consciously versus automatically, aligning outer experiences with deeper priorities in calmer clarity. Simple meditation like awareness of breath or body scan cultivates presence, supporting other techniques' effectiveness for manifestation.

Self-Reflection

Taking occasional breaks reflects on personal meaning, priorities, growth areas, and life's purpose with compassion. It means honestly examining whether daily activities align with core values and long-term well-being versus temporary pleasures alone. Self-reflection identifies unconscious barriers standing between the present and the envisioned future, like unresolved issues from past hurt. Facing shadow aspects with courage creates space for new qualities, enhancing whole-person wellness. It also recalibrates manifestation objectives, ensuring they remain truly reflective of what matters most for living fully with dignity and purpose.

Incorporating various manifestation techniques tailored to situations empowers concrete results. Consistency allows naturalizing skills for spontaneous challenges, while celebratory acknowledgments of achievements keep progress enjoyable and motivation high. With practice, badass mindfulness transforms into a way of conscious living attuned to life's cooperative spirit.

Creating a Personal Manifestation Toolbox

Each person's manifestation journey is unique, tailored to their circumstances and natural inclinations. Rather than following a strict routine, creating your own personalized toolbox of techniques allows you to flow optimally with your desires and talents. This custom approach fosters sustainable motivation, honoring individuality for the greatest results.

Let's explore how to thoughtfully curate methods that assist unique goals in authentic ways. Remember, manifestation is a creative practice requiring experimentation to find what energizes you! While some suggestions await, trust intuitive guidance-seeking experiences that feel just right. With an open mindset, any technique can contribute value when applied appropriately.

Factors to Consider

When selecting techniques, first assess inner resources and outward responsibilities. Consider energy levels, busy schedules, natural interests, and learning styles that impact practice regularity. Don't overwhelm limits or rush spiritual development, which requires patience, not deadline pressure. Identify focus areas that stimulate growth without stressing capacities that are still maturing.

Also note personal preferences like social approaches versus solitude, conceptual focus or sensory elements, intellectual nature, or heart-centered qualities. Your toolbox may prioritize options aligned with conditions permitting full expression. For some, journaling works well, but visualizations feel unnatural. Respect your truth and find harmony.

Beyond traits, examine manifestation aims and milestones motivating practices. Career goals warrant project-oriented methods, while relational visions emphasize cultivation through bonding. Maintaining health involves techniques that integrate practices seamlessly, enriching everyday flow instead of duty. Vary needs seasonally as well, adjusting supports throughout changes.

Trust that guidance for your highest good leads to experimenting with many avenues and seeing what nourishes with the least resistance or contrivance. No single tool alone manifests desires anyway. Diverse angles permit versatility in navigating challenges holistically without reliance on any technique as a super-magic solution alone. Freedom-to-evolve approaches motivate continuous growth, rightly stewarded.

Guidance for Experimenting

Commit to trying several techniques for periods, like a one-month minimum, to decently gauge experiences beyond initial assessments. Note how each impacts thoughts, moods, embodiment, and worldly outcomes, reflecting alignment with deeper truths. Track intuitive hunches that feel like personal empowerment boosts instead of external demands alone.

Customize methods creatively as inspired. Adapt templates from books to personal situations instead of exact imitation. Blend techniques synchronously too; journaling daily gratitude may follow guided imagery practice for a calming transition. Variation maintains interest, while reinforcement compounds small shifts into bigger manifestations through coordinated learning curves.

Discuss toolbox options reflecting desires for accountability and expanding perspectives. Community deepens by sharing life lessons gleaned through diverse manifestations for mutual empowerment. Requests from others also open gratitude for diversity within humanity's shared gift exchange.

Note achievements, big or small, from any practice to stay motivated. Celebrate wins while also reflecting humbly on continued growth with compassion for yourself and others walking parallel roads. Each step expands the realization that manifestation itself is a joyful celebration of life's endless potential within.

Some Toolbox Possibilities

Here are suggestions for experimenting, with no obligation to make any. Simply listen within regarding resonances enlivening manifestation from an inspired place:

- **Journaling:** gratitude, dreams, affirmations, project planning, quotes, and creative stories

- **Breathwork:** pranayama, meditation, yoga, tai chi

- **Affirmations:** spoken, mirrors, vision boards, music

- **Visualization:** guided, drawing, movement, nature

- **Reflection:** self-study, mentors, journals, and creative outlets

- **Community:** masterminds, volunteering, social networks

- **Spiritual practices:** prayer, rituals, blessings, and ancestor veneration

- **Movement:** dance, sports, walks, gardening, hiking

- **Expressions:** writing, art, cooking, crafting, singing

- **Nature:** horticulture, wilderness, water, stargazing

Trust that the process itself guides you toward ever-deepening alignment with life's flow. With patience and faith, your personal manifestation toolbox cultivates wisdom from within for navigating each step authentically. Focus on the intrinsic rewards of the journey, and all other fulfillments will follow accordingly!

My Favorite Manifestation Exercise

My favorite manifestation exercise is the breathing exercise with the body scan and the anchor visualization at the end. I call it a "body scan with an anchor." It starts with deep belly breathing, where I focus only on inhaling and exhaling into my belly. As I breathe, I lie down comfortably on the floor using a yoga mat.

Once I feel calm and centered with my breathing, I begin the body scan. I direct my attention to my toes, taking a moment to notice any sensations without judgment. Then I move to my feet and do the same. I continue slowly moving my attention up my body—legs, hips, stomach, chest, shoulders, arms, neck, and finally to my head.

At each part of my body, I pause for a few seconds to quietly observe any feelings. I don't try to change anything; I just watch with curiosity. Once I've moved through my whole body, I return focus to my breathing again.

After one full body scan, I try to feel my whole body all at once while still centered on deep breathing. All the different sensations from each body part become one united feeling within me. Sometimes, during the body scan, I like to imagine my whole body filling up with a warm, soothing light.

When I reach the head, that's the signal that it's time for my anchor visualization. I clearly picture a symbol that feels positive and empowering to me in front of my mind's eye. Mine is a beautiful golden cat, sitting calmly. Your anchor could be anything that makes you feel good.

I hold the vision of my anchor symbol in place while continuing to breathe steadily. Then, I mentally speak positive affirmations to it, like I'm telling the symbol my goals, plans, and intentions for the day. I express gratitude that it will help keep me on track.

After finishing with my symbol, the exercise is complete. However, throughout the day, if I feel stressed, doubtful, or discouraged, I'll take a moment to once again visualize my anchor in my mind's eye. Seeing it immediately calms my thoughts and lifts my mood toward confidence and strength.

This customized manifestation ritual has proven very useful. It started as a way to overcome a sports fear, but now it helps me face any challenges from a place of power and inner peace instead of anxiety or weakness. The soothing breathing, body awareness, and empowering anchor make it a whole-body experience for cultivating positive outlooks and outcomes.

Conclusion

Throughout this journey of understanding badass mindfulness, we have explored many concepts, techniques, and strategies. Now it is time to reflect on how to integrate all that we have learned to successfully manifest our goals and desires.

Badass mindfulness is a holistic approach that involves working with our thoughts, emotions, and energy and taking intentional, aligned action. It is not enough to just think positively or use visualization techniques. We must address blocks at multiple levels: thoughts, beliefs, emotions, energy, trust, and control issues. The techniques discussed aim to do just that by raising self-awareness, releasing resistance, cultivating positive emotions, and aligning all aspects of our being with our intentions.

One of the most important things we learned is that our thoughts directly influence our emotional states and reality. While positive thinking can help to some extent, true change happens when we become aware of thought patterns and reframe limiting beliefs. This is where journaling, affirmations, and thought-work techniques are invaluable. They help shine the light of awareness on deeper thought processes so we can unpack hidden beliefs and replace them. As neuroscience showed us, new neural pathways form when we think of new thoughts consistently. This changes our subjective experience of reality over time.

Another core theme was the interplay between thoughts and emotions. We saw how difficult emotions like fear, doubt, and resistance arise from certain thought patterns and beliefs. Additionally, emotions influence thoughts in a reciprocal relationship. This is why developing emotional intelligence through practices like self-awareness, empathy, and emotional regulation is so important for manifestation. We must get good at identifying how we feel and what triggers those feelings, as well as having strategies to shift emotional states when needed.

Expressive exercises, mindfulness meditation, yoga, and energy work help with this process of recognition and release tremendously.

Trusting the process of manifestation and embracing uncertainty were also uncovered as vital principles. When we are too attached to outcomes or timelines, we impose resistance without realizing it. Learning to let go of perceived control and just go with the flow was shown to increase manifestation. Rituals for release and surrender, gratitude practices, and cultivating a mindset of uncertainty all help instill trust that things will work out as they need to. We detach from desperation and are open to receiving it in due time.

Mental practices were explored to literally rewire the brain for manifestation. Visualization, mental rehearsal, and energy alignment techniques integrate our intentions into the subconscious mind, where true creation happens. Sustained use trains the mind to automatically follow the imagined path. Symbolism like vision boards and rituals further cements these patterns neurologically. Combining such practices with techniques to break limiting beliefs makes the inner world conducive to outer manifestation.

Vulnerability was recognized as an empowering catalyst. While scary, embracing vulnerability ushers in emotional healing and connection, which in turn support manifestation. Expressing ourselves through writing, art, and music releases old pain stored in the body. This frees up energy previously locked in wounds or trauma, allowing for fresh creative expression. Practicing daily gratitude while being vulnerable to joy and appreciation also feeds manifestation.

With all these multifaceted pieces now in place, the next step is to thoughtfully craft a personal manifestation toolbox, integrating your unique strengths, needs, and lifestyle. Factors like schedule, interests, and energy levels must be considered. It is best to start small by picking a few aligned techniques to weave into the days, weeks, and months. Experimenting with different combinations and adjusting as needed ensures steady, sustainable progress, not quick fixes or burnout. Maintaining a record of learning along the way prevents stagnation or backsliding.

Manifestation is as much an art as it is a science. Going forward, true work is living consciously according to this transformational framework while also giving ourselves permission to stumble gracefully. Transformation happens through dedication to daily practice, not perfectionism over results. With patience, consistency, and creativity, the previously impossible can become a reality. I hope the concepts and tools explored have ignited in you an inspiration and ability to consciously create your life. Trust that you have all you need within you already; now is the time to holistically nurture and express your inherent light. I wish you joy and fulfillment on your journey ahead.

I hope this book has helped you on your own path to purposeful living by providing inspiration and direction. If you have a moment, please leave a review to share your opinions with other readers who might be interested in this subject. I value your input so much because it motivates me to keep getting better and giving my audience interesting stuff. Again, I want to thank you for your help!

References

Antanaityte, N. (n.d.). *Mind matters: How to effortlessly have more positive thoughts.* Tlexinstitute. https://tlexinstitute.com/how-to-effortlessly-have-more-positive-thoughts/

Bailey, K. (2018, July 31). *5 powerful health benefits of journaling.* Intermountain Health. https://intermountainhealthcare.org/blogs/5-powerful-health-benefits-of-journaling

Beringer, B. (2022, January 16). *6 rituals for manifestation that energy workers swear by.* Bustle. https://www.bustle.com/life/manifestation-rituals-energy-workers

Brogley, G. (2020, October 24). *The psychology behind manifestation.* The Campanile. https://thecampanile.org/22670/science-tech/the-psychology-behind-manifestation/

Cherry, K. (2023, October 20). *Mihaly Csikszentmihalyi biography.* Verywell Mind. https://www.verywellmind.com/mihaly-csikszentmihalyi-biography-2795517

Chestnut, K. (2024, January 5). *Connecting mindfulness and manifestation: Enhancing your reality with awareness.* KatharineChestnut. https://katharinechestnut.com/connect-mindfulness-manifestation/

Collins, N. (2018, June 13). *Stanford researchers explore how the human mind shapes reality.* Stanford News. https://news.stanford.edu/2018/06/11/four-ways-human-mind-shapes-reality/

Davis, T. (2023, December 3). *What is manifestation? Science-Based ways to manifest.* Psychologytoday. https://www.psychologytoday.com/us/blog/click-here-for-happiness/202009/what-is-manifestation-science-based-ways-to-manifest

Desk, D. (2023, July 20). *The power of manifestation.* Clinikally. https://www.clinikally.com/blogs/news/the-power-of-manifestation-unleashing-the-phenomenon

8 negatives of positive thinking | amen clinics. (n.d.). Amen Clinics. https://www.amenclinics.com/blog/8-negatives-of-positive-thinking/

Gabriele, T. E., Hall, C. R., & Lee, T. D. (1989). Cognition in motor learning: Imagery effects on contextual interference. *Human Movement Science, 8*(3), 227–245. https://doi.org/10.1016/0167-9457(89)90008-0

Health, A. (n.d.). *Activation meditation: Techniques for energy alignment.* Aura. Retrieved May 9, 2024, from https://www.aurahealth.io/blog/activation-meditation

Jeannerod, M. (1995). Mental imagery in the motor context. *Neuropsychologia, 33*(11), 1419–1432. https://doi.org/10.1016/0028-3932(95)00073-c

Johns Hopkins Medicine. (2019). *The power of positive thinking.* https://www.hopkinsmedicine.org/health/wellness-and-prevention/the-power-of-positive-thinking

Kehoe, J. (2023, September 28). *8 subconscious mind exercises to unlock your potential.* Mind Power. https://www.learnmindpower.com/subconscious-mind-exercises/

Kihlstrom, J. F. (2008). Placebo: Feeling better, getting better, and the problems of mind and body. *McGill Journal of Medicine, 11*(2), 212–214. https://www.ncbi.nlm.nih.gov/pmc/articles/PMC2582657/

Kong, J., Huang, Y., Liu, J., Yu, S., Ming, C., Chen, H., Wilson, G., Harvey, W. F., Li, W., & Wang, C. (2021). Altered functional connectivity between hypothalamus and limbic system in fibromyalgia. *Molecular Brain,* *14*(1). https://doi.org/10.1186/s13041-020-00705-2

Koosis, L. A. (2023, May 24). *The science of affirmations: The brain's response to positive thinking.* MentalHelp.net. https://www.mentalhelp.net/blogs/the-science-of-affirmations/

Melkonian, L. (2021, December 7). *Why vulnerability will change your life: The power of being yourself.* Betterup. https://www.betterup.com/blog/vulnerability

Mind-body connection: What is it and how to strengthen it — calm blog. (n.d.). *Calm Blog.* https://www.calm.com/blog/mind-body-connection

Mindfulness: The power of mindfulness as a manifestation trigger. (2024, April 20). FasterCapital. https://fastercapital.com/content/Mindfulness--The-Power-of-Mindfulness-as-a-Manifestation-Trigger.html

9 interesting facts about your subconscious mind - gail marra hypnotherapy. (2021, November 11). Gailmarrahypnotherapy. https://www.gailmarrahypnotherapy.com/9-interesting-facts-about-your-subconscious-mind/

Oschman, J., Chevalier, G., & Brown, R. (2015). The effects of grounding (earthing) on inflammation, the immune response, wound healing, and prevention and treatment of chronic inflammatory and autoimmune diseases. *Journal of Inflammation Research, 8,* 83. https://doi.org/10.2147/jir.s69656

Paterson, R. (2021, July 19). *Think less and grow rich – richard paterson.* Think Less and Grow Rich. https://www.thinklessandgrowrich.com/thoughts-and-thinking/

Perry, E. (2023, June 15). *5 steps to create a vision board that does its job.* Betterup. https://www.betterup.com/blog/how-to-create-vision-board

Sanfey, J. (2023). Simultaneity of consciousness with physical reality: The key that unlocks the mind-matter problem. *Frontiers in Psychology, 14.* https://doi.org/10.3389/fpsyg.2023.1173653

Schwartz, T. (2012, June 6). *The art of letting go.* Harvard Business Review. https://hbr.org/2012/06/the-art-of-letting-go

6 steps to breaking your limiting beliefs. (n.d.). PushFar. https://www.pushfar.com/article/6-steps-to-breaking-your-limiting-beliefs/

Tello, M. (2019, February 14). *A positive mindset can help your heart.* Harvard Health. https://www.health.harvard.edu/blog/a-positive-mindset-can-help-your-heart-2019021415999

The power of setting intentions & how to set mindful ones. (n.d.). Calm Blog. Retrieved May 9, 2024, from https://www.calm.com/blog/setting-intentions

The Recovery Village. (2023, July 12). *Rumination.* https://www.therecoveryvillage.com/mental-health/rumination/

Vilhauer, J. (2020, September 27). *How your thinking creates your reality.* Psychologytoday. https://www.psychologytoday.com/us/blog/living-forward/202009/how-your-thinking-creates-your-reality

Wood, K. (2022, June 14). *How to harness the power of meditation, mindfulness, and manifesting.* Mindfulness Exercises. https://mindfulnessexercises.com/how-to-harness-the-power-of-meditation-mindfulness-and-manifesting/

Printed in Great Britain
by Amazon